# The General Contractor

## How to Be a Great Success or Failure

By Joe Egan

Bridge Publications, LLC

The General Contractor
How to Be a Great Success or Failure

Published by Bridge Publications, LLC

First edition, March 2012

ISBN - 978-0-9851544-0-0

Printed in the United States of America

To my brother, Jim, for courage and perseverance.

# Acknowledgments

*Editing*
Beth Wallace, Joseph Gentry, and Adam Swenson

*Critique and Support*
Dean Korthof

*Webpage Design*
Wendie Pett

*Photography*
Tim Pearson

*Book Cover*
Robin Krauss

*Cartoonist*
Jennifer Allen

*Patience*
My Wife

# Table of Contents

Chapter One
**The Industry** . . . . . . . . . . . . . . . . . . . . . . . . . . . . . . . . . . . . . . . . **1**
    Dogged Persistence . . . . . . . . . . . . . . . . . . . . . . . . . . . . . . . . 6
    Respect and Realization . . . . . . . . . . . . . . . . . . . . . . . . . . . . 7
    High Expectations of Oneself and Others . . . . . . . . . . . . . . . . 8
    Honed Negotiating Skills . . . . . . . . . . . . . . . . . . . . . . . . . . . 10
    Unconventional Assessment Thinking (UAT). . . . . . . . . . . . . 12
    Humanitarian Efforts . . . . . . . . . . . . . . . . . . . . . . . . . . . . . . 13

Chapter Two
**The Customer** . . . . . . . . . . . . . . . . . . . . . . . . . . . . . . . . . . . . . . **19**
    Logical and Emotional Buyers . . . . . . . . . . . . . . . . . . . . . . . 19
    Creating Relationships . . . . . . . . . . . . . . . . . . . . . . . . . . . . . 24
    Emotions . . . . . . . . . . . . . . . . . . . . . . . . . . . . . . . . . . . . . . 28
    Customer Relations . . . . . . . . . . . . . . . . . . . . . . . . . . . . . . . 32
    The One Hundred-Point Scale . . . . . . . . . . . . . . . . . . . . . . . 44
    Terminate Existing Customers . . . . . . . . . . . . . . . . . . . . . . . 50

Chapter Three
**The Leaders** . . . . . . . . . . . . . . . . . . . . . . . . . . . . . . . . . . . . . . . **51**
    Establish Strong Values. . . . . . . . . . . . . . . . . . . . . . . . . . . . . 57
    Write Simple, Clear Mission Statements . . . . . . . . . . . . . . . . 59
    Choose Your Leadership Style: Hands On or Hands Off? . . . . . 61
    Create Internal Alignment . . . . . . . . . . . . . . . . . . . . . . . . . . 63
    Watch Out for the Division Within . . . . . . . . . . . . . . . . . . . . 66
    Plan for Growth . . . . . . . . . . . . . . . . . . . . . . . . . . . . . . . . . 68
    Use Your Influence . . . . . . . . . . . . . . . . . . . . . . . . . . . . . . . 72

Prepare for Failure . . . . . . . . . . . . . . . . . . . . . . . . . . . . . . . . . . 74
Ease Pressure and Stress . . . . . . . . . . . . . . . . . . . . . . . . . . . . . 75

Chapter Four
**The Subcontractor** . . . . . . . . . . . . . . . . . . . . . . . . . . . . . . . . . . . **77**
Principles of Success in Dealing with Subcontractors . . . . . . . . 83
Why and How to Terminate a Subcontractor . . . . . . . . . . . . . 87

Chapter Five
**Relationship Success** . . . . . . . . . . . . . . . . . . . . . . . . . . . . . . . . **93**
Build Relationships . . . . . . . . . . . . . . . . . . . . . . . . . . . . . . . . 94
Let the Customer Bring Up Business First . . . . . . . . . . . . . . . 98
Use the Customer's Name . . . . . . . . . . . . . . . . . . . . . . . . . . . 99
Be Trustworthy . . . . . . . . . . . . . . . . . . . . . . . . . . . . . . . . . . 100
Listen to Customers . . . . . . . . . . . . . . . . . . . . . . . . . . . . . . 103
Empathy . . . . . . . . . . . . . . . . . . . . . . . . . . . . . . . . . . . . . . . 105
Build Rapport . . . . . . . . . . . . . . . . . . . . . . . . . . . . . . . . . . . 106
Maintain Relationships . . . . . . . . . . . . . . . . . . . . . . . . . . . . 108

Chapter Six
**Relationship Failure** . . . . . . . . . . . . . . . . . . . . . . . . . . . . . . **121**
Betrayal . . . . . . . . . . . . . . . . . . . . . . . . . . . . . . . . . . . . . . . 121
Blowing Up Bridges . . . . . . . . . . . . . . . . . . . . . . . . . . . . . . 124
Betrayal Reactions . . . . . . . . . . . . . . . . . . . . . . . . . . . . . . . 127
False Accusations . . . . . . . . . . . . . . . . . . . . . . . . . . . . . . . . 128
Failure Tips . . . . . . . . . . . . . . . . . . . . . . . . . . . . . . . . . . . . 129
Lack of Tact . . . . . . . . . . . . . . . . . . . . . . . . . . . . . . . . . . . . 132

Chapter Seven
**Presentations** . . . . . . . . . . . . . . . . . . . . . . . . . . . . . . . . . . . . **135**
Why Do Contractors Lose the Award? . . . . . . . . . . . . . . . . . 137
Why Do Contractors Get the Award? . . . . . . . . . . . . . . . . . 138
Effective Persuasion . . . . . . . . . . . . . . . . . . . . . . . . . . . . . . 139
Body Language . . . . . . . . . . . . . . . . . . . . . . . . . . . . . . . . . . 141
Before the Presentation . . . . . . . . . . . . . . . . . . . . . . . . . . . . 142

During the Presentation . . . . . . . . . . . . . . . . . . . . . . . . . . . . . . 147
Present According to Your Roles . . . . . . . . . . . . . . . . . . . . . . . 148
Use and Observe Body Language . . . . . . . . . . . . . . . . . . . . . . . 150
Maximize Your Speaking Skills . . . . . . . . . . . . . . . . . . . . . . . . 151
What Not to Do . . . . . . . . . . . . . . . . . . . . . . . . . . . . . . . . . . . . 152
Use the Emotional Buying Motivators . . . . . . . . . . . . . . . . . . 154
After the Presentation . . . . . . . . . . . . . . . . . . . . . . . . . . . . . . . 158
If You Are Not Selected . . . . . . . . . . . . . . . . . . . . . . . . . . . . . . 159

Chapter Eight

**Boiling It Down** . . . . . . . . . . . . . . . . . . . . . . . . . . . . . . . . . . **161**
Adjust Your Attitude . . . . . . . . . . . . . . . . . . . . . . . . . . . . . . . . 163
Take Time to Make Time . . . . . . . . . . . . . . . . . . . . . . . . . . . . 166
Leave the Job at Work . . . . . . . . . . . . . . . . . . . . . . . . . . . . . . . 167
Perseverance and Purpose . . . . . . . . . . . . . . . . . . . . . . . . . . . . 168
Do Good . . . . . . . . . . . . . . . . . . . . . . . . . . . . . . . . . . . . . . . . . . 169
Share Your Gifts With People . . . . . . . . . . . . . . . . . . . . . . . . . 171

**About the Author** . . . . . . . . . . . . . . . . . . . . . . . . . . . . . . . . . **175**

Chapter One

# The Industry

A s you know, the construction industry is one of the oldest activities created by human beings. It started at the beginning of mankind thousands of years ago when we developed the ability to reason: the cognitive ability to draw a conclusion based on the experience or use of tools or other available material. With such new brainpower, the conscious early man reasoned that rocks could be transformed and used as a tool and thus built the first condominiums, then called caves.

Ever since, construction has been a reflection of a society's technology and values. We know that much has changed and much has not. Tools, equipment and the amount of knowledge are in a constant state of change. There have been major leaps in technology. Slide rules have been replaced by calculators. Blueprints have been replaced by computer-aided design (CAD) and building information modeling (BIM). The plumb bob and tape measure have been replaced by laser beams.

Safety has advanced from being a low priority to a primary concern. The Federal Occupational Safety and Health Act was not signed into law until 1970 and many contractors considered some rules just a burdensome cost increase. Prior to OSHA, construction companies and employees were pretty much on their own regarding the importance and practice of safety. Today, successful companies don't treat their safety representative as a detective who exposes dangerous conditions and scolds workers. Instead the position is high on the organization chart because of the respect they have earned and the realization that safety is about affecting human behavior in the wise (safe) or unwise (dangerous) decisions that we make.

Certainly many things remain unchanged. Road building started about 4,000 B.C. Six thousand years later, roads are still made out of available natural materials and are used for the parallel and perpendicular passage of vehicles powered by animals or motors. Cement dates back to at least 500 B.C. when it was used on a large scale by Roman engineers. Bricks are still laid on top of each other to form the sides of buildings, as they were in 7,500 B.C. Limestone, granite, and gypsum were used to build the Egyptian pyramids and are still being used today. Glass is still made of sand and remains the avenue for views from the inside and it also allows for light to penetrate from the outside.

Quality continues to be a test in knowing its definition and meeting its expectation. Quality has its own separate definition in the world of construction. *The Merriam-Webster Standard Dictionary* defines quality as "superiority in kind."

That definition implies that doing or paying more equals superiority, and therefore greater quality. I believe the definition of quality in the world of construction is "adherence to requirements." It is not simply that an implementation of better or best equals superiority.

An example of construction quality would be in the comparison of one building having a specified requirement for a wall to be constructed with cheap plywood and another building having a specified requirement for the more expensive brick. If the cheaper plywood was installed with good workmanship at the required length and width, then it would be considered a quality installation because it adhered to the requirements. Likewise, if the more expensive brick wall was not installed with good workmanship and did not meet the specified length and width, it would not be considered quality because it did not adhere to the requirements. Quality also continues be a subjective interpretation of what's in the mind of the beholder (the observing customer) and the beholden (the obligated contractor).

Success in construction depends on common factors no matter where you live or what type of construction services you provide. The factors for success are consistent whether you are an architect, engineer, general contractor, subcontractor, or material supplier. They apply if your company is big or small, young or old.

So what are these factors? Common traits for great success as a general contractor include these:

- dogged persistence even when it is easier to just give up and take the easy way out
- respect, realization, and great skill in handling people
- high expectations of oneself and others
- honed negotiating skills to assure a win-win rather than a lose-lose
- unconventional thinking, an outsider mentality, and the guts to march to a different drummer
- humanitarian efforts

Perhaps most importantly, successful contractors are trusted and trusting. Yes, you can be financially successful by not being trustworthy, but that is not what defines success in this book. Instead, being untrustworthy is one of the main prerequisites for failure.

Despite all those positive attributes, the construction industry continues to be one of the least-favored careers. This conclusion is based on my interviews with high school counselors and also on Andrew Strieber's piece, "The 10 Worst Jobs of 2011" written for careercast.com, where seven of the least-favored jobs were directly related to the construction industry. Some high school career counselors are hesitant to encourage students to pursue a career in construction because they know little about it. They may also fear the backlash from parents, who might be offended if they believe that the suggestion is a result of their children's failure to qualify for a higher-status profession.

Those who view the construction industry from the outside often see it as dangerous and dirty with restricted employment opportunities due to cronyism and nepotism. Even the gate signs at the job sites say "Do Not Enter."

The failure of a construction company to survive is caused by three things: a sudden void of a key president or manager without a succession plan; a major financial loss on a large project; the chronic degradation of attitude and discipline from bad thoughts leading to bad temperaments which lead to bad actions.

Construction is not for the faint of heart. It takes strong egos and thick skin. Contractors are faced with contracts that anticipate failure rather than success, with an alphabet full of negative legal language including:

| | |
|---|---|
| Arbitration | Mechanic's lien |
| Breach of contract | Notice of default |
| Claim | Owner failure |
| Damages | Plaintiff |
| Error | Quality differences |
| Fraudulent | Rejection |
| Governing | Subpoena |
| Hold harmless | Termination |
| Injury | Unconscionable |
| Judgmental error | Variance |
| Litigation | Warrantee |

The construction industry is also difficult because there are few people who can thrive on the treadmill of urgency that dispenses constant deadline and revenue pressure while simultaneously demanding swift decision making in a competitive arena. As James Moynihan of Henry International points out in *Engineering News Record*'s book, *Horizons*, "It requires a unique combination of math, personality, psychology, intelligence, common sense, architecture, engineering, and project management as well as hard mental and physical work." Despite all the gains in technology, the construction industry remains relationship-driven. People might think that construction is mostly about brick and mortar, but in fact it's as much about relationship as any business. There are few people who are proficient at both the technical and the relational aspects of construction, yet being good at both is necessary to succeed at, and enjoy, the business.

Although construction processes have changed over time, the humans at the center of the construction industry have not changed that much. In construction, relationships include trust and betrayal, pleasure and pain, satisfaction and disappointment. These all lead to the ultimate success or failure at the end of a construction project, and that is the point your reputation will be measured for success or failure.

That, in turn, leads to whether or not your company will be invited to the next project. Reputation is worth more than money because, without a good reputation, your company may not be granted an opportunity to make money.

It is this human interaction, nearly unchanged through the history of construction, that is the focus of this book.

Contractors have a consistent need to adapt to both good and bad change, to deal with people and their opportunities and problems, to roll with punches, and make hay when the sun shines. It is a unique industry where you can be surprised about things but should not be shocked.

---

**Harry Morrison (1885-1971)**
Morrison worked so hard that his tireless energy actually bothered some people. He was called "that damned kid" but at the age of twenty-seven he formed Morrison Knudsen Company. He promised Knudsen he would offer plenty of guts if he would fund the $600.00 required to start the company. His company pioneered the joint venture approach for the construction of the Hoover Dam and during the 50s was the world's largest heavy contractor.

---

## Dogged Persistence

Construction requires toughness, persistence, and risk taking. It's the will to succeed: not the unreasonable, overly-optimistic Pollyanna approach, just a strong drive.

Competition is such that second place is reserved for the first loser. Survival requires the resiliency of a rubber band snapping back from being stretched. You can allow only a brief period of remorse after being bested from a project award before you must extend your efforts again to get the next project. It hurts to try hard and still experience failure, and the cycle can be relentless.

On the other hand, the business gets you hooked on the rewards of hard work, pride in accomplishment, and valued relationships. It's akin to the outcome of the quotation by Mark Knopfler: "Sometimes you're the windshield; sometimes you're the bug." Thomas Edison, who was involved in construction, said: "I have not failed. I've just found 10,000 ways that won't work."

**Mary Hurd (1925- )**
Hurd had the persistence and conviction to succeed even though her male peers patronized her when there were very few women engineers. She wrote a publication called *Formwork for Concrete*, which is still considered a resource on the subject. She also received a scholastic award for her thesis on welding continuous railroad rails.

**Clifford Holland (1883-1924)**
Using dogged conviction to make up for his youth, at the age of thirty-six he was the youngest chief tunnel engineer in the U.S. and perhaps in the world. After working for the Rapid Transit Commission in New York, he advanced to design the twin twenty-nine foot diameter, cast iron-lined tunnels going between New York and New Jersey.

## Respect and Realization

Successful contractors realize that customer loyalty is not automatically granted: it is earned. They understand that project management is very important, but customer relationships are more important. They know that their best strategic plan includes respect and problem solving, and the worst strategic plan is finger-pointing and betrayal. They are also mature enough to realize that problems do not go away, but do provide a great opportunity to look good when they are solved. Meanwhile, competitors are always waiting in the wings. They watch you for you to make a misstep. They wait for the opportunity to fly in after you've crashed and take away your customers.

The more you know, the more you realize how ignorant you are. Every day, new discoveries transform what was once exciting and nearly unbelievable into obsolescence. I recall when, after spending my first seven years in construction, I reached the level of knowing enough to be dangerous.

I also learned early on that projects that start well usually end well and projects that start badly usually end badly. Getting off on the wrong foot makes it hard to get back on the right one. Good or bad outcomes are many times caused by the manifestation of the self-fulfilling prophecy. You will act in a manner and carry the attitude to justify your predicted outcome. If you believe the project team hasn't earned your respect, you will treat them accordingly, and your thinking will be confirmed. If you believe the project team is your only avenue for success, then you will treat them accordingly and your thinking will be confirmed. One prophecy is doomed for failure and the other prophecy is destined for success. Respect, communication, and building relationships are keys to success in construction.

**George Goethals (1858- 1928)**
Thanks to his great skill in handling people, Goethals was trusted and successful as the lead engineer for the Panama Canal and was able to complete the project despite the futile efforts by many before him.

**Peter Kiewit (1900 – 1979)**
Peter Kiewit and Sons company is one of the largest contractors in the world with projects including the Interstate Highway System, Trans-Alaska Pipeline, the Eisenhower Tunnel, and the Flaming Gorge Dam. He said, "Loyalty is a quality of the heart and cannot be bought."

## High Expectations of Oneself and Others

Success in life is about the constant creation and achievement of expectations. Setting expectations leads to motivation. Achieving expectations fosters pride and confidence to start the cycle over again: create, achieve, create, achieve.

How boring would it be if you no longer had any goals for yourself? High expectations allow you to separate from the pack and make them try to catch up to you. They are self-authored for the purpose of either directing yourself or influencing others. When you achieve your high expectations in relation to your customers, the result is an enhanced perception of the concept of *customer*. Your customer becomes not just some unknown person who pays you money, but rather a respected person you look forward to talking to. Many successful customer engagements evolve into close personal friendships. You may go on vacation together or attend family birthday parties. They may become someone you can share more intimate life details with, be they good, bad, or ugly.

High expectations also result in measurable benefits to the company and the industry, including leapfrog technology and procedures. For example, companies whose high expectations led them to early implementation of AutoCAD, and later building information modeling, reaped the benefits of these improvements in technology. Those who elevated their safety procedures to conform with *Zero Injury Techniques*—first published by the Construction Industry Institute in 1993—are reaping the benefits of greater safety due to their higher expectations. Even though injuries are an unfortunate fact of life in construction, it does not mean that they are acceptable.

Companies with higher expectations for better internal and external relationships have an edge over their competitors. They also show higher productivity, increasing the value of their services to their customers. High expectation is a discipline that keeps you from the temptation of just doing okay. Keeping up with your competitor, but not doing anything better, will eventually lead to failure. Achievement of high expectations forces competitors to say, "Why didn't we think of that?" Legend Peter Kiewit said: "I do not choose to be a common man. It is my right to be uncommon: if I can, I seek opportunity not security."

In the construction industry, activity does not necessarily equal results, yet many people work endless hours to exhaustion without much accomplished. This is not what I mean by high expectations. Companies that have a culture of "who can work the most hours" create burnout at work and stress over relational conflicts within the employee's families.

These both lessen productivity and eat away at relationships internally and externally. Managers can embarrass themselves by running around the office acting busy on self-appointed minor assignments that should have been delegated to others. Compliance in terms of safety, schedule, quality, and budget are difficult achievements and must be high priorities for success. Before you brag about meeting these goals, the achievement only affords you equal comparison with most of your competitors.

Too much activity, including high costs spent on advertising and fancy collateral, may boost your ego but does not always result in the high expectation of contract awards. Fifteen minutes of charm may get you in the door, but skill is necessary to keep you there. I have never heard of anyone getting a contract because they had the nicest brochure.

Remember the last construction-related brochure you reviewed? You probably scanned the pictures of buildings and equipment that were not much different from your photos. You probably didn't read any of the text because you assumed it was all self-serving language. Now go look at yours and see how special it may be to another reader and how well it fits with your customer experience. Does it meet the threshold of high expectation?

---

**Steve Bechtel Sr. (1900-1989)**
After succeeding his father, Warren, who founded the company, he built Bechtel Group into a global construction giant with projects including the Hoover Dam and pipelines, refineries, and nuclear energy.

**Joe Strauss (1870 - 1938)**
He vowed to build the biggest thing. As chief engineer for the Golden Gate Bridge he set a record for tower height and suspension span. He spent eighteen years overcoming political, regulatory, financial, and construction hurdles at a cost of $35 million.

---

## Honed Negotiating Skills

Successful negotiators realize that they may need to give up something they want in order to get what they need and they require the same mindset on the other side of the negotiation table. During a construction project, it is a certainty that unforeseen conditions and situations will arise. Often they lead to some sort of disagreement or conflict because people on both sides have different opinions, perspectives and expectations. There are many ways to resolve conflict including negotiation, arbitration, mediation, litigation and near assassination. Yes, assassination—as you will read in chapter four, I once had a pistol pointed at my forehead during an argument over a change order.

Of all the methods, negotiation is the most efficient and of mutual benefit. A negotiation is simply a discussion intended to produce a middle ground agreement over a dispute. Negotiation gets you through a problem: both sides may not get what they want but they do get all or most of what they *need*. It's a dance with both sides knowing it takes two to tango.

In negotiation, both sides have respect for the existing relationship and want to preserve it. The reason you showed up is about money and if you leave with success it's because there was a win on both sides. In any negotiation, information is power, so you'd better have a good memory and plenty of facts to support your position. A positive attitude and the willingness to be honest in admitting failures are prerequisites in order to maintain the relationship after the closure of the conversations.

Good negotiation requires being attentive to your fight-or-flight impulse—keep your emotions intact. (This works best when you are prepared to count to ten or take a break outside without slamming the hinges off the door.) Be prepared and willing to give something up. Such a concession will allow the other party to feel like they've earned something and got a piece of you even though you may have been willing to give it away for free.

**Jack Lemley (1945 - )**
Lemley started out driving heavy equipment and used his honed negotiating skills in his rise to high level positions for several large contractors. He led one of the first successful large-scale alternative dispute resolution (ADR) procedures for Morrison Knudsen Company.

## Unconventional Assessment Thinking (UAT)

It doesn't cost anything to think in unconventional ways to arrive at new assessments. Unconventional assessment thinking (UAT) is about getting out of the rut of your usual business mode and allowing yourself to see your world from a higher elevation. Permit your head to absorb rather than deflect the new ideas and opportunities that often blaze past you while you're stuck in the rut mode.

Maybe it's because we tend to think more about stabilization and security and not enough about growth and opportunity, but it was UAT that got us through the rut of thinking the world was flat and led to countless inventions including the automobile, the rocket, and modern medicine. In construction, this thinking provided engineered wood products, reinforced and precast concrete, air conditioning, fire protection, LED lighting, and building information modeling (BIM) to name a few.

If you think like everyone else, all you can expect is to match what they are thinking and doing . . . no higher or better. Find a time and place far removed from your urgent world. Have the courage to just sit and be alone with your thoughts. UAT does not come from being on a committee —rather, committees produce dependent thinking based on consensus. Think openly in private and challenge opinions (both yours and others). The point here is not just to be contrary, but to escape the "normal." Get on the other side of the fence and observe what others can't see—or refuse to see—because it is different, challenging, and uncomfortable. Get in the right environment for this thinking.

A friend of mine is an architect for hospitals and clinics. His preferred design for a waiting room is floor-to-ceiling glass with chairs facing toward the windows rather than an interior space where chairs are facing each other. His reasoning is that when people are inside and facing each other, they tend to think internally and more about their personal concerns. If they look outside, however, they tend to think outwardly and less about themselves.

Support UAT in your organization. Suppose an employee was staring out the window while at work and his boss asked what he was doing. The employee responded, "I'm thinking." If the boss is smart, he'll smile and say, "Good. That is what I am paying you to do."

After being turned away from Toyota Motor Corporation, Soichiro Honda was not dissuaded. Rather he embraced possibility and opportunity, and formed Honda Corporation. He said, "We see the world not as it is, but as it could be. We see the world through the eyes of dreamers."

Many contractors eventually fail to succeed because they work just to keep up with their competitors. "Just keeping up" is often difficult given all the risks and competitors in the industry. Those who dare to go further with an outsider mentality and the discipline for UAT are better suited to envision the future and thus succeed into it.

**Elsie Eaves (1898- 1983)**
Eaves was an independent-thinking trailblazer who helped women become more prominent in the workplace. She was one of the first women to graduate from college with a civil engineering degree and also was the first female associate member of the American Society of Civil Engineers. Elsie was also a founding member of the American Association of Cost Engineers.

**William Mulholland (1855-1935)**
Known as the greatest water engineer of the early twentieth century, he built an aqueduct comparable in length to that of ancient Rome's. A pioneer in tunneling, this self-taught engineer completed the 233-mile Los Angeles Aqueduct in 1913.

## Humanitarian Efforts

Success in construction is equally dependent on supporting your fellow man and woman through humanitarian efforts. Doing something to benefit other people gives you balance and helps you realize how lucky you are. Actually taking part in a humanitarian effort—volunteering at hospitals, helping in natural disasters, or directly assisting families of those serving our military—can be very meaningful.

The greatest humanitarian groups I've had the honor in dealing with are those who volunteer in hospice care and the Patriot Guard Riders. I believe in angels and think those who work in hospice care are earth angels. My younger brother, Jim, for whom this book is dedicated, passed away in a hospice home. He was only forty-nine.

Through their compassionate hearts, the hospice staff transformed what we had envisioned as a scary, frustrating and painful experience into a peaceful and comfortable end of his life.

The Patriot Guard Riders (PGR) is a national group, mostly motorcyclists, who have organized to protect those attending the funerals of veterans. The PGR protect and comfort the mourners by forming a wall while holding large American flags. Many members are Vietnam veterans who were spat on and mocked as they returned home from combat, yet they are still willing to stand the flag line with other PGR members to show honor, dignity and respect for our fallen heroes.

Opportunities for humanitarian service can take many forms. In another example, the president of my hometown hospital once called on me for a humanitarian effort.

He explained that parents of children in the intensive care unit (ICU) had to sleep in waiting rooms, sometimes for weeks, because there was no lodging nearby. The hospital president asked if I would reconstruct the interior and exterior of an old duplex next to the hospital into a first-class dwelling.

I said, "Sure, I'll be happy to take on that project. How much do you want to spend?"

"Not a dime," he said. "We have nothing in the budget for this, even though it will probably cost $250,000. I'm asking you to do this for free."

Without hesitation I said yes. I assured him that he would be proud and the guests would be comfortable upon completion of the renovation. Then I called on my friends who owned construction companies for help. They each agreed to do their part free of charge. We created blueprints for the project and presented our ideas to the director of the ICU.

We explained how the existing 1950s-era duplex would be converted into a warm, homey cabin retreat. Parents who stayed there would feel as if they were in the middle of the woods, even though they would be just across the street from their children in the ICU. The ICU director was silent. I looked at her. She was crying, filled with gratitude for the effort and knowing the families would be comforted.

The second bout of tears came at the end of the project. A young boy in the ICU who'd had his legs shattered in a farm accident said, "Thank you for letting my mom and dad have a place to stay close to me." That time, I was the one who cried.

Construction companies have the people, tools, equipment and know-how to build humanitarian projects. If you take these projects on, they will widen the hearts of employees and reinforce your company values. They will also have a distinctive impact on your reputation.

**John Dunn Sr. (1893-1964)**
In 1943, Dunn's company received a contract to build a quartermaster depot for the Army Corps of Engineers. As a WWI veteran with two sons in the military, he refused to profit from the war and requested that the Corps of Engineers reduce his contract to pay for job cost only.

If there were a prescription pill bottle to imitate the construction experience, its label would read:

**Usage:** Take daily for the achievement of personal and business success. Find opportunities and earn victories through the encouragement of accomplishment and despite the discouragement of struggle.

**Side Effects:** Persistence, resiliency, optimism, confidence and pride. Other effects may include irritability stemming from unproductive people, nervousness just prior to bid time, and hair loss from major disputes.

**Warnings:** Avoid exposure to pessimists or those who can't be trusted. Do not take if afraid of hard work, high risk, or big challenges. Stop taking when you have to drag yourself to work.

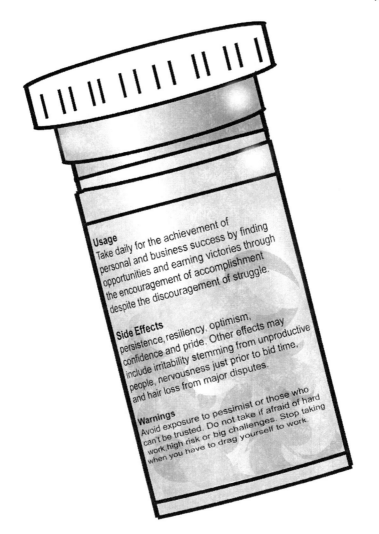

**Usage**
Take daily for the achievement of personal and business success by finding opportunities and earning victories through the encouragement of accomplishment despite the discouragement of struggle.

**Side Effects**
persistence, resiliency, optimism, confidence and pride. Other effects may include irritability stemming from unproductive people, nervousness just prior to bid time, and hair loss from major disputes.

**Warnings**
Avoid exposure to pessimist or those who can't be trusted. Do not take if afraid of hard work, high risk or big challenges. Stop taking when you have to drag yourself to work.

# Chapter Two

# The Customer

W hen I started in the construction business with my father, he told me, "People do business with the people they want to do business with. Somehow they find a way. The trick is to find that way."

In this chapter I'll talk about what you can do to help your customers find the way to work with you, even when your work comes at a premium price. I'll discuss the difference between logical and emotional buyers, building relationships to convert your customers into emotional buyers, and the ten emotions your customers must feel in order to work with you over and over again. Finally, we'll talk about customer relations: the long-term strategies for building relationships that will keep your company in business.

## Logical and Emotional Buyers

No matter what is being purchased in this world, including construction services, there are two types of buyers—the logical buyer and the emotional buyer. Logical buyers tap the left brain, which thinks in words, numbers, parts, specifications, and sequences. The left brain is bound by time. Emotional buyers use the right brain that thinks in images—intuitively, imaginatively and creatively. The right brain is the seat of conscience and hunches, and is not bound by time.

In the fourth century, Aristotle contended in his treatise, *De Anima,* that there were five senses: sight, smell, hearing, taste and touch. In addition, I believe there is a sixth sense that I describe as the "inner voice" or "gut feeling." I describe that sense as the ability to instinctually jump into the future, make an observation, then jump back to the present and make a conclusion and reaction to accommodate what you have sensed.

I believe this sense empathy evolves from either a very stressful experience like posttraumatic stress disorder (PTSD), and is thus a learned behavior, or from a very long relationship with someone that allows you to subconsciously observe and interpret body language and emotions other than your own.

Gut feelings, hunches and your inner voice are evidence of intuition rather than rationality. They are unconscious reflexes delivered through instinctive feelings. They produce a common sense perception of what is the right thing to do about a given situation, even though there may not be any rational explanation or physical proof. The phenomenon remains a mystery that psychologists have yet to figure out, even though intuition is used by most successful people. Here's what some very influential people have to say about intuition:

- "Listen to your intuition. It will tell you everything you need to know." Anthony J. D'Angelo (1974 -  )
- "All great people are gifted with intuition. They know, without reasoning or analysis, what they need to know." Alexis Carrel (1873–1944)
- "Every right decision I have ever made has come from my gut. Every wrong decision I've made was the result of me not listening to the greater voice of myself." Oprah Winfrey (1954–)
- "You can't connect the dots looking forward. You can only connect them looking backwards. So you have to trust that the dots will somehow connect in your future. You have to trust in something: your gut, destiny, life, karma or whatever. Because believing that the dots will connect down the road will give you the confidence to follow your heart, even when it leads you off the well-worn path." Steve Jobs (1955– 2011)

Contractors exercise intuition when they receive a surprise phone call from a prospective customer they want to do business with, yet have not been invited to bid a project. Intuition is exercised to determine if the prospective customer is serious about actually doing business or if you are being lulled to provide a check number for your competitor. More intuition is required when that prospective customer provides the budget for the project: is that amount provided so you can match it and thus receive the contract, or is it a wasted effort to confirm the accuracy of the budget? How do you assist your intuition in figuring out the answers? (For more reading on body language refer to chapter seven.)

Contractors also exercise intuition when they attend pre-bid conferences. These are typically conducted by the owner, owner representative, and architects, among others, and include a question and answer period.

The contractors exercise intuition when they observe how their important and pointed questions are answered. Were the answers forthright and complete, or evasive half-answers? Intuition will provide a positive inspiration or a negative apprehension about bidding.

A pointed question and answer for intuition to respond to could be: "Is there a project schedule?"

Forthright answer: "Yes, the schedule is aggressive and you should include contingencies to assure the project will be completed on schedule. Our consultant has prepared a detailed CPM schedule which is available for your review."

Evasive half-answer: "We don't have a schedule and figure we'll just work it out during construction."

The type of response to that question is what provides the strong hunch or gut feeling about the eventual outcome of the project, hints at whether it will be a promising opportunity or not.

Intuition is also exercised when contractors are first introduced to prospective customers. These are typically semi-formal, get-to-know-you meetings. Here first impressions are lasting impressions. During and after the meeting, intuition will pick up on the high or low levels of comfort, eye contact, concentration and seriousness. This helps you decide if this looks like a great opportunity for a long-term relationship or if there is just something inside that says this is not going to work out.

One example of my sixth sense comes from my experience of being sideswiped on a highway by a pickup truck while riding my motorcycle at sixty-five miles an hour. After the collision I skidded over two-hundred feet before I came to a stop. Years later I still suffer from permanent hip damage, but I also have a sixth sense of when another driver will veer into my lane.

My wife notices this sense when we travel in our car together. When I sense that a car is going to veer into my lane, I slow down and my wife asks why I am slowing. I tell her I suspect the car is going to veer into our lane and, sure enough, it does. That sense is my ability to observe the posture of the vehicle heightened by the very stressful situation of being sideswiped on a motorcycle.

Another example of the sixth sense comes from my forty-year relationship with my wife. Sometimes she pauses in the middle of the sentence, distracted or lost for words—most of the time I am able to finish her sentence verbatim.

Some people may describe these events as coincidences or lucky guesses but I believe it is a deeper extraction of intuition and predictability. Albert Einstein once said, "The only real valuable thing is intuition."

So why is that sixth sense so important when dealing with your customer on bid day?

You want your customer's sixth sense to give him a gut feel and a hunch that he is better off giving you the contract even though you may not be the low bidder. You don't want his sixth sense to tell him not to give you the contract even though you have fulfilled the bid requirements and are the low bidder.

Men are less intuitive than women because we have largely been taught to be logical and not show emotions. Men are thus more likely to make decisions based on facts, or at least to justify their intuitive decisions with facts. At the job sites and at the office, the construction industry is male-dominated. Most of the decision-makers in construction are men. It is therefore more of a challenge to convert your left brain, logical-decision-making construction customer into a right-brain, emotional decision maker.

When purchasing your construction services, the logical buyer will deduce that Company A has a fee of five percent and Company B has a fee of seven percent. Left-brain logic tells him that five is less than seven, and therefore the award should go to Company A. The emotional buyer, using the right brain, will deduce: I know that five is less than seven but I also know that the two numbers are very close and something inside me—my inner voice and my hunch—tells me I'll be better served by paying a small premium to award to Company B.

What helps the customer access this intuition? It's your relationship with the customer and your ability to help the customer visualize the successful completion of the project. The positive emotions stemming from the relationship influence the customer's decision to award you the project, even if your price is higher. They trust you and your work, therefore, they choose you.

An example of logical and emotional buyers outside the construction industry comes from the purchase of men's shoes. Each store offers the same product—a right and left foot, each having a heel and toe, with options for lace-up or loafer. The majority of colors are black and brown. Some people go to a discount store and make a logical decision to purchase a pair of size ten black loafers for $40. Other people go to a high-end store, such as Nordstrom, and make an emotional decision to purchase a pair of size ten black loafers for $120. Yes, there is a difference in material quality, but I believe most of the three-hundred-percent difference in price comes from the feeling of the positive experience rather than the feel of the leather.

Why? How? An element of Nordstrom's marketing plan can be summed up this way: "Nordstrom does not emphasize price, but rather a series of elements that makes the shopping experience. Once you get the customer excited, they will want to come back to you."

Those elements are the positive impressions you receive over the phone or in their store which motivates you to pull out your credit card—even when you might be able to get a similar product at a cheaper price—because price is not what Nordstrom emphasizes. It's not about how much money you save, but rather how good you feel once you have made the purchase, and how satisfied you are with the end result.

Nordstrom's strategy wouldn't work if you didn't have a great experience or if the product was shoddy and fell apart within a month.

While writing this chapter I called Nordstrom's customer service center and asked the question: "What makes Nordstrom special?"

Without hesitation, Nicky replied: "Our customers expect so much from us and we are empowered with the freedom to do anything reasonably possible to make sure our customers are happy. That freedom is also why I love working here."

I hung up and called the same number back and asked again: "Why is Nordstrom special?"

Again, without hesitation, Jake said: "I put myself in our customer's shoes when they have a problem. I just don't do the minimum, I go above and beyond. I don't give up and most of the times I'm successful, and that makes me happy."

I hung up and called again with the same question. Bren replied: "That's a big question, but it starts as soon as you walk in the store. Our people know what they are talking about. It's not like some other retailer where they have to go find someone else to answer your question. We also have individual flexibility to help our customers and we don't have to ask permission to do it."

What kind of experience does your customer have working with you? If your customer randomly called one of your employees, would they answer in a similar way? You can apply Nordstrom's philosophy to the widgets you install, whether it is concrete, steel, brick, doors, or walls.

## Creating Relationships

So how do you convert your customers from logical buyers to emotional buyers? You create relationships with them. You help them get to know and trust you and your company.

I have a friend who is the business development manager for a general contractor. He was asked by his boss to prepare a marketing plan. Typically this means creating a three-ring binder with glitzy brochures, self-serving compliments about the company, and facts and figures about safety, quality, and ability to meet schedules. This kind of marketing plan is time-consuming and expensive to create, and often makes one company look no different from its competitors.

When my friend was asked to produce his marketing plan he pointed to two pieces of paper on his wall. The top page read: "Marketing plan." The second page read: "Get out of the office and meet with your customers." This is the first step toward building relationships.

Think about it: have you ever negotiated a contract because you have a neat brochure and a cool website? Or, instead, have you negotiated contracts from the basis of strong emotional ties? Which contracts have served you best? Which projects have been the most enjoyable to work on? Which have brought you the best return?

Your customers desperately want to be understood on an emotional level. Emotions are a person's involuntary, subjective, and internal state of being. To understand and respond to someone else at an emotional level requires empathy—the ability to feel, and understand, the emotions of others. When people feel heard and understood, they are more likely to trust. When your customer feels understood, they trust you, and they are willing or even motivated to give you the award whether or not your bid is the lowest.

Don't believe me yet? It is at this point in some of my seminars on this subject that I get a glassy stare and hear comments directed at me like: "You just don't get it, the only thing that matters in the construction business is low price." If that is what you truly believe, then you are perfectly correct. Low price is often the criteria for public bids, but not always. If you are only thinking about providing the lowest price, you can easily ignore the other critical buying factors.

For a nuclear power plant, high-quality products and installation methods are a bigger buying factor than low price. For a refinery, extra labor hours to assure safety are a bigger buying factor than low price. For a project with liquidated damages, extra labor is a bigger buying factor than low price. Low price does not assure that a bid is responsive to the customer's concerns, or even responsible.

In most cases, the human relationship is more important than the technical requirements. Customers want your services, but they also demand a positive emotional experience and a high level of professionalism. That special place is what's beyond just budget adherence and meeting specifications.

Customer motivations are the things they need or want. *Needs* are what the customer has to have for the project to be successfully completed. *Wants* are the things they might be able to afford if the budget allows. Customers' needs and wants fit into four general categories: things they want to save, increase, reduce, or improve.

## Save

Typically customers want to save time, money, effort, or resources. If saving time is their main concern, you may hear them say something like: "This has to be ASAP . . ."If saving money is primary, they may say: "I need to build this within my budget." If wanting to save effort, they may say: "I want this done without any hassles." If saving resources is on the top of their list, they may say: "I don't have the time or people to do this myself."

## Increase

Customers may want to increase income, investment, or relationships. If they want to increase income, they may say: "I want to increase revenue with this building expansion." If they want to increase investment, they may say: "This new building will increase our real estate portfolio." If they want to increase a relationship, they may say: "I am disappointed with the last contractor and need someone I can trust."

## Reduce

Customers often would like to reduce liabilities, trouble, and expenses. If they want to reduce liabilities, they may say: "I need a contractor who can work safely in this environment." If they want to reduce trouble, they may say: "The last contractor caused me more harm than good." If they want to reduce expenses, they may say: "That building is costing us too much money to heat."

## Improve

Your customers may want to improve appearances, their peace of mind, the company's productivity, or their capacity. For example, if they want to improve appearances, they might say: "I need a better-looking office building," or "The outside of this building looks terrible." If they want to improve peace of mind, they may say: "When this critical project is complete, I will be able to sleep again." If they want to increase productivity, they may say: "Customer service needs to be relocated close to the warehouse so they can check up on shipments if necessary."

These examples of customer needs are also their buying signals. When you hear these statements, you know what is important to the customer beyond price. These are clues that tell you what the customer is willing to spend money on. They seem obvious and very simple to detect, yet it is surprising how many contractors totally ignore those buying signals and instead formulate their own false assumption about what will trigger the customer to buy from them. It's as if they place a veil over their eyes in order to not see the buying signals.

Those contractors ignore the importance of overtime payments when liquidated damages—that high price penalty for not meeting schedule—are involved. They ignore the requirement for higher quality of work when appearance is important. They ignore the extra safety requirement when danger is inherent. They end up not getting the contract when the customer says: "You just don't understand the scope of work or what we expect of you." It's not always about low bid, so take the box off your head and listen to the buying signals.

The relationship with your customer should be thought of as a bridge—you are on one side and your customer is on the other. The reason for the bridge is to establish a long-term relationship so that, over time, you become the customer's builder of choice. Also you want him to be promoting your business name when he is talking construction with his business contacts.

The foundation of the bridge is the positive emotions in your relationship. This is a bridge that takes years to form and build. Your employees are the stewards of the bridge and must manage and maintain when problems arise. Everyone in the company has the ability to blow the bridge up. This could happen in a flash, before you know it, when the wrong thing is said to the wrong person at the wrong time. If the bridge is well-built and if it has been carefully maintained, it will take more to blow it up than if the relationship is crumbly and poorly-maintained.

## Emotions

Your emotional-buying customers are motivated to award construction contracts for two reasons: to solve problems and to feel good. There are ten primary emotions you want your customer to experience in their relationship with you and your company. Experiencing these emotions consistently over time will serve you well as you build and maintain your business relationship. This is not touchy-feely, hand-holding, Kumbaya philosophical mush: I am talking about a disciplined and refined level of service.

In addition, helping your customers to experience these ten emotions will help you achieve personally and help you discover the secrets of business success.

Personal success is not exclusively about making huge sums of money. It is also about the value you create for yourself and others when you know that your hard work has paid off.

These are the ten emotions you want your customers to experience:
- comfort
- anticipation
- optimism
- desire
- pleasure
- amazement
- pride
- happiness
- relief
- passion

## Comfort
Comfort is your customer's feeling of freedom from having to be bothered about what might happen. It's being content in a state of ease and wellbeing. Your customer is able to sleep well, aided by the comfort and security of knowing he is in good hands.

A customer who expressed comfort with his contractor said: "I don't think I would have made it through without you. You have the patience of a saint, thanks. Your honesty was extremely comforting."

## Anticipation

Anticipation is your customer's excited feeling that something good is going to happen; the condition of eagerly looking forward to something. Your customer is expecting you to fulfill all that is required as he contemplates and visualizes the future.

A customer who got what he expected from his contractor said: "Your knowledge and professionalism went beyond our expectations. We realized this from day one."

## Optimism

Optimism is your customer's trusting belief in the best possible outcome. An optimistic customer dwells on the most positive aspects of any situation with the belief they will look good at the end of the project. It's a trusting and cheerful confidence in predicting the future.

One customer who was optimistic about his contractor said: "When I think of the word trust, I think of them. I don't know exactly why, but I trust them."

## Desire

Desire is your customer's craving for satisfaction. It's a burning emotion that motivates a person to transfer thought into the act of achieving the goal. Your customer desires to get the job done with no hassles.

A customer who had his desire satisfied said: "We love how you work—you listen, you offer helpful suggestions. What can we say; we are really grateful for your help and love your style. You're the man!"

Note: The previous emotions of comfort, anticipation, optimism and desire were about the customer's anticipation of the future. The following emotions are reactionary to your customer's present activity.

## Pleasure

Pleasure is your customer's delight that an accomplishment has been made. They also may feel gratification that pain has been avoided. Meeting your customer's preference or choice gives them a feeling of enjoyment and delight. Your customer will have pleasure and peace of mind when things are going well. This is a feeling that your customer feels is worth seeking again.

A customer who received pleasure from his contractors said: "I don't have any words to express the dedication of your team. They fixed my problem right away just when I was struggling."

## Amazement

Your customer feels amazed when they are surprised by something good they didn't expect. This is a pivotal emotion in the relationship bond: you can amaze your customer by going the extra mile when problems arise, or you can amaze them by doing something very stupid and dangerous. Either way they are filled with amazement.

A customer who was amazed at his contractors said: "You totally impress us! You are completely on top of your game. We aren't easy to please and you never disappointed us or let us down."

## Pride

Assuming the "amazement" emotion was positive, you advance to the emotion of pride. With this emotion, the customer actually feels proud and dignified. Because of your accomplishments they are allowed to feel increased self-respect and self-esteem. Why? Because they were smart enough to choose you for the project.

A customer who was proud of their contractor said: "Thank you so much for being such an awesome person. Anyone would be lucky to have you helping them!"

## Happiness

Happiness is the state of wellbeing and contentment that arises when your customer thinks of you. Happiness is something that everyone wants from life—it allows your customer to be easygoing and a better communicator. It makes it easier for him to get up in the morning knowing he will be dealing with you. This is where you not only have a great business relationship but also genuine friendship. This phase in the progression of emotions would be a good time to plan a vacation together or some other personal event where you can share your happiness.

One customer who was happy with his contractor said: "Over the course of several months, we discovered that you are truly a wonderful person."

## Relief

This is the second-to-last positive emotion that occurs at the end of a successful project. The relief comes when your customer no longer feels a particular stress or burden because the job was successful. This happens because something or somebody—hopefully you—alleviated the stress. Your customer feels relief because the job went well: you didn't take advantage of his vulnerabilities, you solved problems without causing him drama or embarrassment, and you treated him more than fairly.

A customer who felt relief from his contractor said: "Buying this building was one of the most difficult and traumatic decisions in my life. You were always one step ahead of my questions and concerns, stepping me through it with the care of a father."

## Passion

One of the strongest emotions, passion is the ultimate emotion you strive for. It is linked to love, joy and eagerness as well as hatred, anger and apathy. Positive passion is your customer's warm and cordial desire to award you the next contract. It's the condition of the hunch and the self-talk being acted upon by positive emotional experiences. Passion is your reward for helping your customer feel all the other emotions. Remember that what you do or don't do on the current project will affect whether you do or don't get the next contract.

A customer who had passion for his contractor said in a letter of recommendation: "If you are debating whether this is the right contractor to consider, you can take your thinking cap off. In the world of construction, they are a true gem."

If your customer feels these ten emotions, they are more than likely to come back to you the next time they have a construction project with the desire and intent to award you the project, even if you are not the low bidder. They are likely to recommend you to other customers. The more of these passionate customers any business has, the larger the business and success can grow.

This level of professionalism is not easy to achieve: many don't have the guts to face failure or the ambition to give it a try. That is why it is so important for you to separate from the pack and take the extra time and effort to develop the relationships and nurture the emotions. The payoffs are great: they include enhanced job security, flattering image among your fellow employees and the ability to negotiate lucrative win-win contracts with your repeat customers. Let the others continue to struggle for low bid status without enough money in the estimate to really serve the customer.

## Customer Relations

Helping your customer experience the ten powerful emotions that keep them negotiating contracts with you is a long-term effort. The ability to transform satisfied customers into loyal customers is a hallmark of long-term success in any business, and construction is no exception to this rule. Any construction company needs loyal customers to ensure a solid base of revenue, a necessity for long-term growth. That company's employees need loyal customers to ensure employment.

Creating high-quality customer experience requires discipline, integrity, motivation, optimism, and persistence. When you pay attention to customer relationships, your customers may not always be able to define the difference between you and your competitor, but they will have a gut feeling that they will be better off with you.

In these companies, twenty percent of the customers provide eighty percent of the revenue, following the Pareto principle (also known as the law of the vital few). The Pareto principle states that, for many events, roughly eighty percent of the effects come from twenty percent of the causes. Companies that do not experience this law of the vital few typically have much higher overhead, which makes them less profitable.

As I write this I can anticipate readers saying I must be living in a different reality. Maybe your company is doing the right things and still not getting contracts unless you are the low bidder. Yes, that happens. It happens when your competitor is also doing the same right things, which neutralizes the emotional buying triggers previously defined in this chapter. If the customer has essentially the same experience with all the companies bidding the project, he will default to the logical buying decision: the low bid. The trick is to have the discipline and perseverance to do more—to build stronger relationships, to provide a higher quality experience with, and for, your customers.

Without that discipline, contractors treat the customer as a neutral character. Without a strong relationship, contractors believe that low price is the sole determining factor for award. That faulty, ill-conceived attitude requires less effort, and no change within the organization. It requires only a short-term and short-sighted commitment to your customer, for the duration of the job. It doesn't ask you to put in extra time to develop relationships. It has only one goal—to achieve the lowest price, which is objective, measurable and simple to explain. Estimators and business development people in a customer-neutral organization have less risk of criticism from their boss for not getting the next contract. It is easy and factual to simply explain they were not the low bidder.

On the other hand, in a customer-focused organization, those employees have much more explaining to do. They are frequently the target of criticism. They may come under fire from employees in the accounting department who want to know why the company is spending so much money on customer relations when apparently being the low bidder is all it takes to get a contract. This is also the main reason why so many construction companies experience stress and discord between the marketing and the administration staff. The return on investment from marketing efforts is difficult to measure in terms of time and results, but the outflow of that money is very measurable.

It is not that customer-neutral or customer-focused companies are better or worse than the other but instead their respective focuses are different. One focuses on the world of concrete actions (estimating and bidding) and concrete results (either you are the low bidder or not). The other focuses on customer relations, a world of ambiguity, where it's harder to determine and measure cause and effect.

Consider another situation that does not compel just the low price. Imagine you are severely sick or injured and call for an ambulance. The buying signal here is high speed, not low price. Once you get to the emergency room, the buying signal is specialized, high-quality care not the low price. Many construction customers fall into a similar category where it's not always just low price. To find the customers with whom you can develop long-term relationships, follow these guidelines:

- Focus on the best customers
- Create relationships
- Get everyone on board
- Provide real service
- Ask customers for feedback
- Terminate your customer when necessary

(Note to reader: From here on out, I will give examples of "How to Be a Great Failure," the subtitle of this book. Failures will occur from both internal and external activities and are an unfortunate reality in our business. My purpose in demonstrating failure is not to undermine our industry, but rather to point out hazards to avoid, neutralize, or eliminate when managing your way through challenge and crisis. I have added cartoons in some examples in attempt to lighten the load of the heavy burden that failures create.)

**Focus on the Best Customers**
To achieve the eighty/twenty rule—where eighty percent of your

revenue comes from twenty percent of your customers—you must narrow the number of customers you can serve. Focus on valued customers that offer you not only a profitable business relationship, but one that enjoys quality as well. Their bid lists are by invitation, restricted to a relative few companies, and are drawn from a prequalification process. Risks are explained and controlled through a contingency process. Contract terms can be negotiated, site conditions are made favorable for labor productivity, and payments are prompt. These customers actually look forward to mutual success, personal relationships and repeat business.

So where do you find them? Everywhere: pre-bid meetings, social events, planned introductions, industry events, seminars, the stranger sitting next to you on an airplane, or the stranded motorist that you stop to help. I assume that everyone I meet could be a prospective customer or is someone who could put me in contact with a prospective.

## Create Relationships

Three types of customer experiences exist in the construction industry. The first experience has adversarial characteristics: all parties involved with the project believe the other parties should be taken advantage of. The second type of experience is that of neutrality of relationships, which exist primarily in the low-bid public market. This is where you come in and do your job and leave with no intent to develop a relationship. You have no motive to harm or assist others. The third type is a relational experience where your customer wants to do business with you because of a deep and lasting relationship that is productive, positive and mutually beneficial.

Any of these experiences can result in financial success on a given project, but the third has significant rewards for both the contractor and the customer, and is the path to long-term financial success for a contractor. This is the type of experience you want to create for your customers.

In the adversarial experience, projects start out by drawing a line in the sand with a permanent marker. Both sides seem ready for a fight and are prepared to win. The locations of these projects are not called job sites—instead they are called battlegrounds. Each person in each company protects themselves and no others. They have no interest, time, or emotion to expend on developing relationships or to assist in solving one another's problems. Instead the strategy is to look for errors instead of answers and to get them before they get you. Customer problems are not viewed as an opportunity to help a partner, but instead as an opportunity to request extra money.

The adversarial experience exhausts your financial resources and your employees' motivation and is often completed in a mediator's office or the courtroom. Many of them result in permanent loss of relationships between all the parties involved. After a project manager completed one such project, I interviewed him about what he learned. "I learned a lot about people on this project, but what I learned the most was how to suffer. I am now stronger and more prepared in the unfortunate event I get involved with another project like this." Unfortunately many contractors have experienced at least one adversarial experience project in our careers. The trouble comes when we think this is the normal (or even the only) way to get the job done.

In the neutral experience, all parties believe that they are neither friend nor foe, and business relationships are unemotional and neutral. This requires only short-term commitments, usually limited to satisfying the customer's basic project needs of safety, quality, and schedule. The bid price does not include contingency money to pay for extra service, quick response, or free change orders. Nor is there a requirement to form interpersonal relationships. When problems arise for one party in the project, others may care, but can't or won't do much to solve them. Instead they simply report the problem but do not take the extra step to provide solutions. The customer's experience is clearly better in this scenario than in the adversarial experience, but it's also not positive enough to create a loyal customer.

In the relationship experience, the customer believes that the contractor is his path to a successful project, and the contractor believes the customer is his path to a satisfying work experience, a fulfilling career, and a paycheck. It's the wise realization that both parties want to be dependent upon the other for mutual success. The wisdom comes from knowing the enemy experience is like war: nobody really wins.

In this experience, everyone in the company understands that quality relationships are where the next contracts come from and they expect to negotiate contracts for the right price, not just the low price. When the customer calls for anything, everyone in the organization jumps—even higher than the customer expected. When estimating projects, the contractor looks for buying signals other than low price. When problems arise during construction, the contractor views them as an opportunity to help a partner and make the project better.

This type of experience is the most rewarding financially in the long-term, and the most satisfying interpersonally, but it requires a different kind of effort. It may take years to develop the relationship culture in a company and to develop relationships with customers. The relationship experience takes the long view.

Each of these three customer experiences fosters a certain kind of company culture. Hiring a project manager who exudes an adversarial experience and placing him on a project with a customer who demands a relationship experience will soon result in the customer's request that he be removed from the project team. At the same time your customer will question your poor judgment and your respect for them. If you want to create a relationship experience company, you have to hire and develop relationship experience employees.

## Get Everyone On Board

If you want to create positive, long-term customer relationships, you must make sure that everyone in your company understands the importance of relationships and makes it a priority. In order to turn satisfied customers into loyal customers, everybody in the company must be selling the company. Everyone must be aligned with the company's idea of what the word "customer" means and the company's philosophy about how to treat customers. Everyone must believe that the customer is a good thing. This sounds simple and obvious, but it is not. How many times have you heard people in your company complain about customers? How often have you done it yourself?

When everyone in the company is not aligned on the topic of customers, the result for the customer is confusion, which could lead to disappointment and a diminished level of respect for your company. In one construction company I know of, one project manager was presenting a construction claim and placed a surprise lien against a customer, while at the same time another employee was trying to negotiate another contract with the same person.

When everyone is not on the same page, some employees proceed on change orders with a verbal directive, while others refuse to proceed without a written contract amendment. Customers receiving such mixed messages will stop doing business with a contractor because of their legitimate confusion about whether the company is in the problem solving business or the "gotcha" business. Is the contractor with them or against them? A properly-aligned culture has to happen within the organization before it can be of benefit to the customer.

The first step in building a relationship-aligned culture is alignment at the top. Upper management must set the example through consistent messaging and personal practice. The employees must not only be supported but also expected to uphold the company value of customer respect and open communication. It should literally be a condition of employment and therefore a central focus of performance reviews.

One construction company had a hypocritical CEO who plastered the walls with trumped-up banners and signs about how to treat the customer in a positive way, yet in meetings with employees he seemed to loathe the word "customer." He made it clear that, to him, a "customer" was a necessary evil that had to be satisfied in order to receive payments. Some observant employees were then taught to mistreat customers as well and to ignore the hypocritical customer service banners. Other employees realized the inconsistencies would eventually lead to total failure and thus left the company for higher ground.

**Provide Real Service**
The word service is thrown around like the word love: it can be

genuine or artificial. The word can be stated over and over again, but the deed may not always follow the word. Many contractors do not realize the importance of providing real service. Real service is extraordinary availability, promptness and reliability. Availability means 24/7, promptness means right now, and reliability means steadfast, consistent behavior. Real service happens when your customer says: "Wow. I didn't expect you to do that much for me that quickly."

There are many ways to provide good service that are ignored by many general contractors. Good service starts with actually having a human being as a receptionist rather than having a computer-generated voice that forces your customer to go through the alphabet on his phone's keypad to reach someone's voicemail. Certain key people in the organization may be "the face" of the company but receptionists are "the voice" of the company.

Another measure of real service is to avoid turnover with project managers and superintendents while on the project. When these key positions turn over in the course of a project, the personal relationship becomes replaced by a stranger, and intimate project information gets lost in the translation. This requires your customer to start the learning curve all over again.

Real service also includes using polite collection practices. Work with your customer on payment issues, not against them. Alienating the person who holds your money through threats or placement of liens will only further delay the payment process.

Real service means never making your customer pre-punch your work. Your customer should never have to generate a punch list. Do it internally both during the job and after the work is installed. An owner's punch list should be considered an embarrassment.

If your company touts a service department for immediate response, then be prepared to backup your word. A good way to frustrate and lose your customer is to have them call you with an urgent need for your service and place them on hold. Imagine your customer's operations are shut down. They call your service department and hear: "Hello, thank you for calling ABC Company, your call is important to us. All of our service managers are busy with other customers. Please hold and your call will be answered in the order it was received."

Your customer then fumes while on hold as he listens to a recorded message stating: "With ABC Company, we provide fast and personal service because you are very important to us. You can be assured that we provide solutions and timely response to your service needs. Please stay on hold to hear more about our effective service."

By now, your customer is thinking, "If I'm so important, why am I on hold?" He soon feels like a fool waiting in an endless line of other fools. Meanwhile others at his company are waiting for his response to urgent questions about when the system will be back in operation.

This is the point where your customer hangs up and calls your competition. Your competitors have been waiting for this call for years. This is their opportunity to replace you and respond as fast as you should have. Guess what? You're out and they're in.

A real service department does not outsource to an answering service, but has an employee who is available 24/7 to receive customer calls. That employee must be familiar with the service department but does not need to know how to solve the problem. Instead that employee simply needs to let the customer know that he is on it and that the appropriate service person will be contacted and dispatched.

Real service stems from the employee attitude of wanting to make things better for the customer rather than being forced to help the customer against their will. It's also the willingness to become subservient and the knowledge that what you *do* is more important than what you *say*.

Regardless, if the customer is acting on emotion or logic, they must have the impression they are going to come out the winner. It's the simple-yet-difficult exercise of listening, making promises, and keeping them within a short period of time.

## Ask Customers for Feedback

Constantly seek customer feedback. Your customer will appreciate the opportunity to either praise or vent. Customer feedback is important, but it's only useful if you are going to act on it. When you make a plan to collect customer feedback, at the same time plan how you are going to make changes based on what you hear.

Feedback can be either through informal or formal methods. The informal method I use each time I call a customer is to say, "Hi (first name). How are you today? Is this a good time to call?" While placing you in a subordinate position, this immediate concern for their wellbeing opens the door for feedback about anything that is positive or negative in their life. It creates a pattern for ease and open communication for future conversations. It conveys your position that what is important is what's about them and not about you.

I recommend two formal methods of gathering feedback: the SWOT interview process, and the one-hundred-point scale.

*SWOT Interviews*

S.W.O.T. interviews ask your customers for honest feedback about your company's Strengths, Weaknesses, Opportunities and Threats. In my experience, many companies go forward blindly with ignorance and false assumption when in the formal process of strategic planning. It can be a wasted process of ready-shoot-aim.

For this reason, I advise companies to conduct full SWOT interviews with customers. I use slightly-modified versions of the questions about opportunities and threats to take advantage of the customers' specialized knowledge that the contractor might not otherwise have access to. Asking the customers to weigh in about your company sends them a strong message that they are important enough to be part of the strategic plan.

A company must be brave in order to conduct a SWOT interview. It can open Pandora's box and embarrass employees from top to bottom. I have witnessed employees being fired soon after the SWOT interview results came in. Those who practice denial do not conduct SWOT interviews. Actually, this is one of the strongest reasons for undertaking the process—if you are willing to hear the truth, SWOT interviews can give you information that sets you on the path to success. This is because you have a teachable spirit and are open to the assessment of your peers.

**Strengths** are the positive attributes (real and perceived) that add value in the mind of the customer. They can include resources, advantages over competition, exclusiveness, people skills, shared values, problem solving, and reputation.

**Weaknesses** are the negative attributes (real and perceived) that detract from your ability to attract or retain customers. They can include poor people skills, lack of expertise, limited resources, better competition, excessive change order requests, poor judgment, conflicting values, and poor reputation.

**Opportunities** are situations that could allow you to prosper. They can include market growth, geographic expansion, ability to offer more services, failure by a competitor, or an unknown project. The "O question" I ask the customer is, "If you ran ABC construction company, what opportunities exist that they are not taking advantage of?" Answers have included: "We have construction projects in other parts of the country that they should get involved with," and "They are good at what they do, and should expand their services."

**Threats** are situations that could place you in jeopardy. They can include better competitors, market turndowns, new regulations, the loss of a major customer, leapfrog technology, and negative press coverage. The "T question" I typically ask customers is: "What could ABC Construction do to threaten the relationship with your company?" Answers have included, "The next time they send us that same foreman it will be the last job they do for us," and "If I ever have to deal with another punch list like that, it will be very difficult to recommend them for another project."

You will be surprised to learn all kinds of things you didn't know through face-to-face interviews with selected customers to determine their perceptions (and therefore perceived realities) about your company. From that you can determine if there is consistency between who *you* think you are and who *your customers* think you are. The analysis will also help to determine if there is an alignment between the premium the customer is willing to pay and what you are willing to put on the table. Creating this alignment obviously makes it easier for your customers to adopt your services.

These interviews should not be conducted by an employee because your customer may not divulge negative remarks out of fear or embarrassment. Instead seek an independent consultant who is familiar with your company and is respected in the industry to conduct the interviews. That person must have great listening skills, plus the ability to hear both good and bad news without an emotional reaction. That person must also be uniquely qualified to process the information in a professional manner.

Do not conduct the interviews by phone. Such interviews are impersonal and appear to be low budget. That situation hinders comfort and the opportunity for open communication.

To have an honest and effective learning experience, don't limit the interviews to your best customers. Instead, select customers that are both impressed and upset with you, as well as prospects that know your company but have not yet done business with you. Interviewing prospective customers is a great opportunity for you to find out what they need in order to start doing business with you. It may be that you discover something that opens the door for future business.

Interviews start with a letter to your customers signed by your most senior officer explaining your interest in their opinion. Inform them about the name and background of the third party SWOT interviewer, and that he will call them to arrange a meeting at their office. Ask them to prepare to answer questions about your company's strengths, weaknesses, opportunities and threats.

Once in the customer's office, the interviewer will start by telling your customer he is there to simply ask questions, listen and takes notes. He should also make it clear that he is a neutral party and state he is not in a position to either glorify good behavior or defend any misbehavior. He should also tell the interviewee that he will keep their feedback confidential unless they agree that they can be identified as the source.

Once all the interviews are complete the interviewer should compile all the remarks by customer and by category. (A sure way to ruin this effort would be to breach the customer's request for confidentiality—therefore confidential statements should be noted in a miscellaneous comment section that does not tie the confidential remarks to any individual who was interviewed.)

When the survey results are issued, be smart enough to disseminate information appropriately. Also be brave enough to be honest with your employees and share all the information, not just the summary and analysis. The only thing to withhold is customers' names if someone asked for confidentiality. Silence may lead employees to assume the worst has happened and you are afraid and too insecure to let them know. In this case, silence is not golden. The strengths or weaknesses could be reputation, attitude, technical ability, market expertise, financial situation, safety and quality. Use the strengths to leverage your company and to motivate and reward employees.

Weaknesses should be considered as lessons learned and not to be repeated, or at least minimized, with the realization that we are still human and mistakes will be made.

Opportunities should be considered as free marketing and sales information. Threats are the forecast of an impending storm for which you need to better position your company to best withstand the buffeting that surely lies ahead.

## The One Hundred-Point Scale

Another way to discover how your company is performing is to have your customers evaluate your company compared to your competitors. This is a one hundred-point maximum test based on ten performance criteria. Each criterion is graded on a scale of one to ten for how your company compares to your competition.

Here are the ten criteria I recommend:

- safety
- quality
- schedule
- communications
- attitude
- estimates
- project management
- administration
- company owners
- integrity, trust

Again, I recommend that this survey be conducted face-to-face, because it is one more way of showing that you really care about the customer's opinion. A typical question under the subject of safety could be: "Compared to our competitors, how do we rate on a scale of one to ten specifically in the areas of mindset and compliance?"

Below is an example of what the scale might look like when filled out by one of your customers. (Note: Company X is your company)

**Sample Scores**

|  |  | Company X | Company X's competitors |
|---|---|---|---|
| 1. | Safety (mindset and compliance) | 10 | 7 |
| 2. | Quality (meeting plans and specifications) | 7 | 9 |
| 3. | Schedule (meeting long- and short-term goals) | 10 | 6 |
| 4. | Communications (tactful and timely) | 8 | 8 |
| 5. | Attitude (positive and problem solving) | 10 | 5 |
| 6. | Estimates (clear and complete) | 10 | 10 |
| 7. | Project management (consistent and competent) | 9 | 9 |
| 8. | Administration (documentation and billings) | 5 | 9 |
| 9. | Company owners (rapport and agreement) | 5 | 10 |
| 10. | Other observations (loyalty, trust, respect, etc) | 4 | 8 |

What can you conclude from a report like this? A quick look at this table gives me the following insights:

- Company X's safety record is good, as it should be

- Company X is better at meeting schedules than the competition but it appears to be at the sacrifice of quality.

- Company X has a better attitude than the competition in dealing with the customer. This might well get them the next job even if they are not the low bid.

- The administrative departments need to be told about the importance of the customer.

- The owners of Company X better get out and meet the customers. If they don't, the project manager will take them along if he leaves the company.

- There is something bad lurking with loyalty and trust that could soon end Company X's relationship with this customer. It would be a good idea to ask further questions in this area, and make amends and reparations as necessary.

## Terminate Customers

Sometimes a contractor must terminate nonproductive relationships with prospective or existing customers, even though it appears contradictory to the financial requirement to maintain both revenue and your existing customer base. In order to focus on your best customers, you must let your worst customers go. Terminating those customers will make your organization more productive and happy because they consume too many of your company's resources and employee's energy and emotions.

Focusing on the good customer relationships demands careful scrutiny of your customer base, accepting only those who pass the relationship test. I'll talk about both of these kinds of customers below, and then I'll give you some tips about ways to terminate customers when necessary.

## Reject Prospective Customers

In order to protect your organization and develop loyal customer relationships, you will also need to pass on some prospective customers before you do business with them. You often meet these prospects through a proactive cold call or an unexpected invitation to bid their project. Usually, something doesn't feel quite right from the beginning. Trust your instincts, and look for the following clues. They may indicate that you should head for the door and never come back. These customers do not deserve your time or consideration. Don't waste your time if there is little or no equity involved.

### Body Language
Look for the avoidance of eye contact, nervous gestures, and other guarded behavior that might indicate that person is probably holding something back and may not be trustworthy. Also, pay attention to how they greet you. Beware of an overly firm handshake, with the customer rolling their palm down and your palm up, thus placing you in a subservient position. Looking you up and down is another sign they feel superior to you.

### Criticism
If they criticize others in front of you they will probably criticize you in front of others. This is an indication that no matter how well you perform, it will not be good enough. They criticize to feel superior and assume the right to make value judgments about you. They are living with anger and frustration over unmet aspirations and like to blame others for that. Critics also feel inferior through lack of self-esteem and feel the need to degrade others in order to elevate their low prominence.

### Disrespect
Keep an eye out for someone who fails to provide appropriate recognition to others. Disrespect is a purposeful action that results in insult or humiliation. Some people like to offend people and also like to break rules in their favor, and therefore have no problem breaking promises or manipulating contract language that was intended to be in your favor. If during your interview they pick up a phone call or multitask, this indicates that your presence is not their top priority.

### The "I" Word
People who say "I built this job" are many times forecasting self-absorption, low ego, and inability to share credit for a job well done. Unless it was a very small project, they are probably lying as well. In order to truthfully say that "I built this job," a person must have personally performed everything including the architecture, engineering, prefabrication and all the construction. Team players can use the "I" word by saying: "I worked on this job."

### Intimidation
If a potential customer brags about how many contractors he fired and the number of claims he has defended, it indicates that you are looking at someone who conceives of a construction project as a win-lose situation. This customer will create an adversarial experience on the job site.

### Too Friendly
These prospective customers are complete strangers yet are overly friendly. Unexpectedly they invite you to bid their project. Often they set a trap in order to lure bidders into a project that is not properly budgeted with an intention to underpay. This can be a situation of "Welcome to my trap."

### Too Vague
Prospective customers who are overly vague about the project often do not intend to award you the contract. Instead, they need a check number bid from you that allows them to justify awarding the project to your competitor who already has a good relationship with them.

### Too Fast
Prospective customers who are in an extreme hurry are often in a panic to receive a bid from you because your competitors are refusing to bid to them and the project is going behind schedule.

When any of these red flags go up and you have to make the decision about whether or not to bid, ask yourself the question: Why are they calling me?

For example, I was involved in such a project where an out-of-state customer called me out of the blue and was overly friendly, vague, and in a hurry. As project manager, I attended the pre-bid meeting which included a tour of the proposed work area. The customer told the bidders that the work area would be free of interference from any of the owner's operations or any other contractors. This positive working condition was then confirmed in writing as part of the pre-bid meeting minutes. Unfortunately, I fell for the trap. Our company submitted a multi-million dollar bid and was awarded the contract . . .

Months later, we mobilized the project as scheduled and were surprised to see an overly-crowded construction site, with over thirty other contractors and hundreds of craftspeople installing various items in our work area. There was not even space for our office trailer or material storage. I wrote a letter to the customer, stating our position of changed conditions and resultant labor inefficiency for which they were responsible. As the conditions had changed drastically from what was represented prior to bid, the customer agreed and asked us to document our payroll cost. At the end of the project they promised to pay us the difference between our estimated cost and our actual cost. We documented those costs and submitted daily timesheets that were signed by the owner's job site assistant.

At the end of the job, we sent them an invoice for $3,200,000.00 in labor cost overruns as agreed due to the suffering labor conditions. As you may have suspected, things turned bad. The owner's representative could not remember that he had said he would pay for our cost overruns. When we submitted documentation verifying the agreement, he was transferred to a different state. When we produced the daily timesheets with signatures from the project assistant, we were informed that he was not authorized to sign or approve anything. We eventually negotiated a settlement under the threat of claiming punitive damages against them through litigation.

Moral: Trust your instincts. If it doesn't feel right, it probably isn't.

## Terminate Existing Customers

How do you know when to terminate an existing customer? Some customers just can't be pleased no matter what you do. They are always demanding that you exceed the contractual requirements for no extra money. They call late on Friday afternoon and expect you to jump through hoops at the job site early on Monday morning. They are unable to manage themselves and blame others for their problems and inadequacies. They prefer intimidation over tact and have no problem causing you to be singled out and demeaned at a project team meeting. They shout and point fingers when demanding action. Their punch lists are an endless evolution of pettiness: later, they demand that you provide free repair on items well beyond warranty.

For them great is not good enough—they overspend your money and emotionally exhaust your employees. Dealing with bad customers may make your dedicated employees resentful and bitter when they feel their good nature and extra efforts are being taken advantage of.

One such customer that I fired converted the saying "If it ain't broke, don't fix it," into "If it ain't broke, then break it." He challenged everything that was done right. Contract performance in the areas of safety, quality and schedule became an endless cycle of not-good-enough. Our project manager was bullied into performing work well beyond the requirements of the contract and the customer was impossible to deal with when requesting change orders for that extra work.

Bad customers find it impossible to cooperate and maintain long-term relationships with contractors. These customers' lack of empathy and compassion leaves them indifferent to the problems of others. They are unable to (and uninterested in) recognizing the feelings of others. Customers like these are willing and equipped with the power and authority to bend the rules in their favor. They will manipulate ambiguous plans and specifications to their favor.

When you are dealing with a customer like this, you cannot create a relationship. They are unable to engage in the give-and-take of an equal relationship. This is the kind of customer you must fire. You can't change them, so don't waste your good intentions by trying to sway their minds and hearts. Consider these customers an occupational hazard. They will injure the financial aspects of your company and the mental well-being of your employees.

There are many ways to terminate a customer: the first rule, however, is not to make a public proclamation. It is best to do it in private without emotional fanfare. I fired one customer because we were unable to make any profit on his projects and he consumed too many of the company's resources. At our final meeting I told him: "With all due respect, I've come to the conclusion that we are not qualified to perform for you, because no matter what we do, it is not good enough. I think you should find another contractor that can meet your expectations." What I wanted to say is, "You will no longer have the enjoyment of kicking us around."

Another way to terminate your customers is to use avoidance and treat them like teeth. If you ignore them long enough they will go away. Use simple excuses to avoid bidding to them. For example, here are some phrases I've used in the past:

"We are too busy and can't take on any more work."

"The A-team that you request is busy on another job."

What is the person we call the customer other than the provider of food on your plate? It's the person who might occasionally drive you crazy with last-minute changes and requests, but overall provides a long-term and harmonious relationship. It's the person who requests free-of-charge preconstruction services while providing an opportunity to generate a fair profit on that next project. It's the person who is willing to be vulnerable to you even though by contract status you are subservient to them.

What is ultimately important is not the brick and mortar you build into the project but what the customer gets out of it.

On the other hand, always consider the wise words of Joel E. Ross: "Never underestimate the power of an irate customer."

# Chapter Three

# The Leaders

L eadership means asking "What do I want to accomplish?"
Management means asking "How do I do it?" Many books
have been written about successful management, so I will not
focus on that in this book. Instead this chapter will focus on leadership
in the construction industry.

Successful leadership of a construction business requires the ability
to have people want to listen to you and to follow you. It also requires
setting two critical priorities: taking care of your customers and
demonstrating strong leadership. If you can put these two priorities
at the top of your list, everything else should fall into place. Strong
leadership creates strong employees who then can provide the business
with strong customer relations. Without strong employees and good
customers, the business is sure to fail.

I do not believe in the concept of someone being a real born leader.
Some people are born into a leadership role simply because they are
the son or daughter of a CEO or king of a country. The subject of
leadership in this chapter is about the constructive performance of
leadership that you are not necessarily born with, but I believe starts
to develop at an early age. Perhaps it's a result of not wanting to be
a follower, but instead being ready to challenge the status quo with
the guts to stand up for what you believe while accepting the risk
of rejection. This desire to differentiate oneself is blended with the
optimism in saying "yes we can" when the pessimists are saying "no we
can't," while having enough personal stock to be self-confident.

Anyone in a construction company can demonstrate leadership. It does not require being a certain age, having a specific type or length of education, having a lofty title attached to your name, or being the best at working on a computer. In fact, many of the great leaders in the construction industry never went to college.

Being a manager, boss, director, or supervisor also does not necessarily equate to being a good leader. In fact, many in the construction industry have witnessed senior managers who are terrible leaders and instead are dictators. Therefore, leadership is a character trait that does not require you to be in a position of power, but it sure is a smart way to get into one.

Leadership in your company can be performed in two separate environments: inside the office with fellow employees, and outside the office with customers. It occurs when employees summon inner strength to set and achieve extra expectations. This is something that can't be demanded of someone but rather is a voluntary act demonstrated by setting an example.

Many of the great leaders in the construction industry started somewhere near the bottom and with little money. They started by pushing wheelbarrows, tending to bricklayers, or mixing concrete. They became leaders because they wanted to: they had enough hands-on experience and were smart enough to know when someone was trying to pull the wool over their eyes. These leaders knew the industry was risky, so they evaluated how much to gamble in a risk/reward scenario. They achieved success by surrounding themselves with competent managers who were motivated and optimistic, and who were often smarter than the leader. They identified their company's values by determining what acts would result in the best interest of employees and customers: honesty, open communication, respect and continuous learning, for example. In doing so, the leaders gained what was in their best interest—namely, a good reputation, loyalty and a healthy compensation plan.

Leadership happens when one person helps others achieve their goals. Leaders of the organization become successful not through self-promotion, but through the assessment and conclusion of the followers in the organization. For example, successful estimators demonstrate internal leadership by seeking methods for increased labor productivity and initiating value engineering ideas. Estimators demonstrate external leadership by being on top of emerging technology to increase the accuracy and productivity of the estimating process.

Project managers demonstrate internal leadership by respecting and honoring the requests and responsibilities of administrative staff. They demonstrate external leadership by being proactive in resolving customer problems or complaints. Those involved with business development show internal leadership by producing proposals that show a clear and elevated distinction from their competitors, rather than the generic, off-the-shelf type of proposal. They display external leadership by constantly being on the positive mind of their customers. Internal and external leadership is what provides increased job security and consideration for promotion. It also gets you the next contract.

Leaders are responsible for setting the vision, being examples for the managers, and then getting out of their way by allowing them to take calculated risks and to make mistakes. In the construction industry, I believe it is smart for leaders to turn their organization chart upside down. In other words, it is the mindset that the people in the office are working for the people at the job site rather than the people at the job site are working for those in the office. This mindset is essential because profits or losses are mostly created by the field and just counted in the office. It is therefore the responsibility of those in the office to assist in maximizing efficiency and labor productivity in the field.

With this mindset, when communications come from the field, the people in the office say, "How can I help you?" Field employees who feel they are on top of the organization chart are proud of themselves and produce very high levels of loyalty and positive attitudes which are reflected when working both with fellow employees and the customer. With that type of leadership, everyone is driving in the same direction with less congestion while getting to the destination of Profitville.

Successful leaders also understand the difference between urgency and importance. Urgency is handling the day-to-day important problems. Urgency is when you have a job site accident, when an upset customer calls, or when OSHA shows up at your door with a surprise visit. It's about what has to be responded to right now!

Importance is about thinking ahead one year, five years, and ten years, and making strategic plans in order to stay in business. Leaders are responsible for concentrating on the important things while delegating the urgent things to those most able to handle them. Project managers and foremen exhibit leadership when they know what their crews will be working on next week and what other work could they be shifted to when that plan fails. Upper management practices leadership by thinking five and ten years down the road about market conditions and succession.

Allowing people to take calculated risks and make mistakes is an important function of the learning curve. Yes, it is risky—but those who have been taught by their supposed leaders through consistent public and private reprimands about their mistakes eventually learn not to take any more chances, regardless of the probability for greater success. To protect themselves from further wrath, they hunker down and become afraid of being assertive. They lose esteem and confidence and are hesitant to raise issues or offer strong opinions.

Instead, they offer multiple suggestions and ask other people to choose which is best. They also become most comfortable being a "yes man" by making suggestions as a member of a committee rather than making independent decisions based on their own judgment. The result of a criticism-based culture is extreme loss of morale and organizational inefficiency in decision making, action and results. Passion can be destroyed by poor leadership.

In order to let the managers take care of the day-to-day urgent matters, leaders in a construction company should have their sights on the horizon. Paying attention to these nine factors will move a leader in the direction of success for the company.

- Establish strong values
- Write clear, simple mission statements
- Know your leadership style

- Create internal alignment
- Watch for division from within
- Plan for growth
- Use your influence
- Plan for failure
- Ease pressure and stress

## Establish Strong Values

Values are the beliefs or philosophies that connect to the heart of the company. They are statements that confirm your company's desire to achieve high levels of performance. Values should be articulated clearly, and the practice of the company's internal and external communities must be aligned with the stated values. Values should be used as a measurement of the company's success. Therefore, rather than a long list of ten or twelve values that sound good but that no one can keep track of, single out three or four primary values that you will adhere to no matter what.

Those values are found from within the company rather than invented by an outside consultant or outlined in a management book or seminar. Nor should your values be copied from your successful competitor. Distinct adherence to values will set your company apart from the competition.

Maintain consistent communication about what's important to you. Don't tell people to go to the left on one day and change direction the next day. Credibility is dashed when your message shifts unpredictably.

Values that are not practiced will be revealed through hypocritical behavior toward employees and customers. Without aligned values, a company has no foundation for employee or customer success. Ignoring the company's values when it is not convenient destroys the legitimacy of your intention to achieve something together without the need for encouragement or enforcement.

For example, if you value "open communication," then throughout the company, employees must accept different or opposing opinions with listening skills and empathy, along with a thank you in appreciation for someone offering their opinion. Employees attempting to practice the value of open communication by giving the boss an alternative suggestion should be met with appreciation and genuine interest, instead of disdain and the reaction of "My way or the highway."

If you proclaim the value of integrity, then the company's leadership must do the right things and practice what they preach even when they are not being observed. A company with the phony value of integrity is able to look the other way instead of righting the wrong, and able to toe the line as far as legality is concerned.

Leaders and managers can produce policies and procedures in an attempt to enforce the company's values, but they will likely not stop anyone who wants to violate them. Instead the practice or non-practice of values can best be seen through the leader's observation of an employee's words and actions. These will demonstrate whether the employee is on board with the company's values.

Many people resist change, and most people's character has long been established. Employees who are not willing to practice the values should be asked to leave the company. Those who are in a position to enforce values and yet turn a blind eye to violations are often themselves seen as void of integrity and character.

Values, even though tough to measure, can also be a selling point for your company. My company was invited by a large healthcare organization to make a presentation for the purpose of prequalifying onto their bid list for future projects. Some of our competitors were also invited.

In preparation I realized I was unable to highlight our company by simply presenting our ability to meet quality, safety and schedule. Our competition was just as good in those areas. So instead, I prepared our team to talk only about our values. I went to the potential customer's website and found their values which were essentially the same as ours, just using different words. Then each team member was assigned a value and prepared to present about how it was similar to a value of our prospective customer. They also discussed how the value was important to each of us in the company and gave an example of how the value was practiced.

At the beginning of the presentation I told the prospective customer: "We could give a presentation here today about how great we are in the areas of quality, safety and schedule—but you probably assume we are able because you invited us here today. Instead we invite a conversation about our shared values. The reason is because we desire a very long-term relationship with you. Success in achieving that goal must first start with what we value. Without shared values we have no chance for a long-term relationship."

Each presenter then described one of the shared values—what it meant to them as an individual and how they would carry it out during construction for the mutual benefit of both companies. Yes, it sounds mushy, but I received a congratulatory call soon after from the prospective customer, who told me that it was the most unique interview he had ever been involved with. He said that we made it very clear that we were not interested in short-term gains for ourselves but instead wanted a long-term, win-win relationship.

Soon after this meeting, we were awarded the first of many contracts, most of them on a non-competitive basis.

## Write Simple, Clear Mission Statements

A company's mission statement should define the purpose for the company's existence. It should be the first consideration and commitment when making a decision. It should be short with meaningful clarity. For example, Walt Disney's mission statement is: "To make people happy."

Unfortunately, many companies have fuzzy mission statements for which they hired an expensive wordsmith consultant. In his cartoon "Dilbert," Scott Adams described mission statements as, "A long, awkward sentence that demonstrates management's inability to think clearly." Using Dilbert's definition I created the following awkward and useless mission statement: "To engage and develop an initiative to continually foster sustained and balanced integrated processes and policies to encourage collaborative solutions using state-of-the-art methods through mutual efforts and endeavors to achieve the goal of customer satisfaction. We are dedicated to achieving these proactive measures which will transform paradigm shifts into the fulfillment of out-of-the-box thinking."

Those words really say nothing and therefore really mean nothing and the efforts taken to produce that mush are wasted. Even though everybody can agree with the words, it gives no specific guidance to drive the decision making. Unfortunately for many companies, their mission statements are written with the most clichéd phrases in the English language.

Another problem with many mission statements is that they do not differentiate the company from its competitors. They do not help the company to stand out either internally or externally. How many construction company letterheads could be affixed to this mission statement? "At XYZ construction we strive to exceed expectations through commitment to safety, quality, and schedule with an emphasis on continuous improvement and customer service."

Instead of imitating your competitor, determine your unique factor and make enhancing it your mission.

I'll bet that many of your employees are unable to recite your company mission statement, because it is too long to memorize or too vague to be relevant. What if you modeled your mission statement on Disney's? Your mission statement could be: "Bid or negotiate contracts; make profits to improve our company and the community." Bidding and negotiating contracts means you are doing something right both internally and externally. That means bidding competitively, not stupidly in hopes that some magical surprise will save your labor budget. Negotiating contracts means you are maximizing your relationships and unique capabilities. Making profits means you can produce payroll and better your internal and external community. If these priorities were followed, then everything else should fall into place.

## Choose Your Leadership Style: Hands On or Hands Off?

There are two ends of the spectrum in leadership styles: hands-on or hands-off. Either extreme can be effective and some prefer to lead somewhere in the middle. Each style has separate rules for success. These are determined by understanding how far the leader is motivated and qualified to get involved, and at what point the managers are motivated and qualified to take charge.

Hands-off leaders establish consensus about strategies, objectives, and tactics and ask questions like these:

• Where are we going? (Strategy)

• How do we get there? (Objectives)

• What are the individual and specific tasks to meet the objectives to accomplish the strategy? (Tactics)

Hands-off leaders then must back away, giving employees the freedom to move forward, make good decisions, take calculated risks, make mistakes, recover, select customers, and develop relationships. If you manage this way, going on extended vacations or enjoying hobbies during the work week is okay because that is part of the rules of your working relationship with your employees. One such leader I knew was honest enough with his managers to tell them: "I'm paying you good money to work hard so I don't have to."

The managers were okay with that because they knew where he stood, and because his leadership style allowed them to take on more responsibility and have more control of their destiny. When these leaders return to the office, they should act like a visitor, because that is what the employees will think they are. They should do the walk-around and greet employees, expressing genuine interest in what they are doing both at work and home.

Good leaders take time to review the current status of the strategic planning process including objectives, strategies and tactics. If you are one of these leaders, don't fool yourself into thinking you wear a Superman cape when you come back to the office. Saying you are going to roll up your sleeves to solve problems previously solved by others could be an embarrassment to yourself and an insult to the employees. During your absences, your employees learned to make decisions and solve problems without your presence. You delegated that responsibility for them to lead and not be led. Remember them dearly when it comes time for bonuses because it is largely their effort that provides your standard of living.

The hands-on style works well for employees who prefer to be led by someone who acts as paternal/mentor figure. This requires nurturing, direction, follow-up and monitoring. With this style, leaders set the strategies and the objectives, and the employees are responsible for the tactics. This organization prefers scheduled performance reviews to determine that I'm okay and you're okay.

The temptation for this type of leader is to micromanage. Even though these employees may not be involved with the formation or implementation of the strategies or objectives, they are responsible for the tactics. That responsibility should not be taken away from them.

One such boss I knew who had a large construction company made the mistake of micromanaging. His intent was to show employees he was "game-on." He wanted to demonstrate his experience and expertise in all company matters, big and small. He would occasionally go into the warehouse and help load the delivery trucks. In doing so he disrupted the work sequence, caused safety violations, and undermined the responsibilities of those loading trucks. Employees in the warehouse would mumble to each other, "Doesn't he have some important management stuff to do?"

A hybrid of hands-on and hands-off management is for the organization that has a leader who is able and willing to be actively involved and also willing to delegate so that someday he will be able to retire with a strong team of managers who became successful under his guidance and support. This style seems most common with general contractors where the first-generation leaders started out doing everything and therefore have the ability and willingness to be involved, yet have grown the company to the point where they must delegate to managers who are also able and willing to carry on to the next generation. The key to success in this style is the leader's willingness to let go. The key to failure is know-it-all micromanagers who don't trust or, worse yet, don't respect the ideas and opinions of subordinates.

## Create Internal Alignment

Construction companies must have positive internal alignment and mutual support whereas businesses in other industries may not and still be successful. For example, those who sell commodities like plastic bags, soap, or erasers to big box discount retailers on a one-hundred percent commission basis may not require much support from others in order to do their job. In many organizations, the only commonalities are the office address, the company product catalog, and the company name on their commission check. In these organizations, those who require support from others, committee decisions, and constant feedback will be frustrated and unproductive while waiting for others to be part of their success.

Contractors have the opposite environment. In construction, the chain is only as strong as the weakest link. Estimators are dependent on those in business development to get on the bidder's list. In turn the development team is dependent on estimators to produce responsible and responsive proposals. All employees are dependent upon the payroll department to get a regular paycheck. The foremen are dependent upon the warehouse and delivery drivers for timely delivery to the job sites. Project mangers depend on the foremen to comply with safety, quality and schedule requirements. It's like traffic on a busy road where thousands of vehicles all have to do the right things at the right times in order to keep an orderly and safe flow of traffic—if one vehicle does something wrong it can negatively affect the progress of many others.

Successful mutual dependency requires respect when having casual conversations in the office. Leaders provide a model of internal alignment or misalignment through their examples of personal behavior and treatment of employees.

Yes, birds of a feather flock together and perhaps they do so for safety in numbers, but leadership requires that you sometimes need to jump out of the flock.

In construction as in the old saying, people who have similar backgrounds—project management, estimating, accounting, computer, or safety—often spend time together. This is also true with religious, racial, and political groups. Maybe they congregate because it provides people with security and comfort in recognition where they are more likely to be accepted. Such segregation limits a person's sphere of influence and knowledge, however. It can also result in prejudice against other groups.

Leaders must not tolerate negative comments about employees from those defined groups who are fulfilling the responsibilities of their links of the chain. Leaders must listen for comments which can pit one group against another, such as:

- "The foremen get all the attention and we work just as hard."
- "We have more responsibility than the guys in the warehouse, but they get paid more."
- "The salespeople get to go out and have all the fun at company expense while we are stuck in the office."
- "Many times we have to stay late at work but the people on the job site always get to go home at 4:30."
- "We are important too, so why can't we get company trucks just like the project managers?"

Leaders must pay attention to and quash negativity and promote cohesion. An example would be a situation where those in accounting are called "bean counters," those in IT are called "geeks," estimators are called "guesstimators," project managers are called "prima donnas," and senior managers are called "white hats."

Successful leaders set the tone of mutual respect with the understanding that everyone has a job to do, so let's do it without backbiting the very people we are dependent upon for success. These leaders help employees realize they don't have permission or the qualification to demean others. This includes appreciating the smiley voice of the office receptionist even though there may be major trouble at her home, or understanding that the safety person may appear overly restrictive and is causing inefficiencies, but he is only trying to protect your safety. It's also about respecting the IT person when your emergency is number ten in line. Those in the company that are in a position to help someone are also in a position to hurt someone. The cost to operate a hurtful company will increase due to the intentional inefficiencies caused by employees getting even with each other.

I observed a CFO once who created a rift between his administrative staff and the sales staff. He had a personal grudge against the sales staff which originated from his examination and reluctant reimbursement of entertainment expenses. This may have been caused by jealousy or someone taking advantage of the perks and lording it over his staff. Not able to find the values in those expenses, he instead considered the efforts in weekend or evening social events with customers as mini-vacations for those salespeople that were paid for by the company which simply added to overhead cost with no tangible benefit.

Clearly, he should have kept his opinion to himself and his mouth shut. Instead he communicated his opinion to his staff that then also carried his negative and destructive attitude in conversations among themselves.

On Monday mornings, these two sides engaged in battle. For example, sometimes salespeople would come to work an hour or so past the normal starting time. Due to family commitments they were unable to attend to during the weekend. Instead, they spent the weekend with a customer. The receptionist would greet him with resentment, saying something like, "You're an hour late. Did your watch break?"

Made to feel doubly guilty about not being with his family and being an hour late, the salesperson would walk down the hall of shame to submit the expense account to the payroll department. There, he'd be greeted by the administrator with the comment: "Oh, it must be great to have your job." The administrators vented their negative attitude, while the salesperson wondered why he did not spend time instead with his family. Likewise the salespeople might not have been aware that the administrators took work home without additional compensation or appreciation. Both sides lost because the group's leaders did not communicate the value of the salespeople being out of the office and the importance of the administrators being in the office.

If everyone feels like they are being treated fairly, they are less likely to be resentful. Poor leaders can breed resentment when they create instability in the way people are treated.

## Watch Out for the Division Within

Some construction companies set up different divisions to match their various markets which demand specialization within that industry. Such divisions might include industrial, commercial, highway heavy, design-build, healthcare, and so on. This market segmentation strategy can be beneficial to your company because it demonstrates your specialized talents. It allows your customers to feel comfortable knowing they have a specialist working for them. In theory, from an accounting standpoint, internal divisions are tasked to assure greater accuracy in allocating overhead and identifying profit centers. They are also beneficial in measuring individual accomplishments and divisional merit.

Unfortunately, when the accounting system pits internal divisions against one another, this strategy creates divisiveness within the company. When that happens, employees change their definition of division from one of "capacity, specialization, and strength" to one of "internal competition." Some may become disenfranchised from the organization and may not be motivated to adhere to company values and the concept of teamwork. This results in collaborative deficiencies among the divisions.

As in the National Football League, all players are working under the "company" but each player is paid to only benefit their team. By the rules of football, players cannot help members of another team, because they are not paid to do so and would be against their individual goals.

They are only getting paid to help their team. When construction companies have similar strict rules against cooperation, they create a situation where, when one employee helps another employee in another division, it can appear to be an act of irresponsibility, or disloyalty to their division. When the divisions are evaluated competitively, loyalty to one's team demands that cost and effort be reserved for one's own division. The company as a whole suffers when divisions and employees are pitted against one another in this way. Trying to be one big happy family may not work, but cooperation must trump confrontation. Getting out of this mess requires an understanding of where managers failed and a path to end it, including termination of those who won't serve as team players.

For example, I knew a project manager who worked for a construction company with several divisions. Each division had its own manager who was responsible for overhead, revenue, profit, and loss. At his performance review, my friend proudly discussed taking a couple of days to help a project manager in another division solve a problem. His manager replied: "Your paycheck comes out of my budget for this division, and I'm not paying you to help out someone else's division!" That project manager entered the meeting with a definition of division as "area of specialization" and left the meeting with a new definition of the word: "separation, discord, demarcation and rift."

Methods of motivating and rewarding employees in divisional companies have been a point of confusion and frustration for all employees, top to bottom. There is no single method of practice. All companies are different in accounting methods and attitudes toward teamwork, and therefore each company must decide on their own if they are going to work together or work apart. Companies that should work together and share profits are those who have divisions that complement each other, such as a painting division and a drywall division. However a company that has an out-of-state industrial division and a local commercial division may not need the divisions to work together.

Some companies have two-tiered rewards systems in which the first bonuses are paid to each profitable division and then a second bonus is paid to every division if the entire company makes a profit with all its divisions. The big conflict comes when five of the six divisions produce a profit, yet all are denied the second tier of bonus due to the failure of one division. One thing in this scenario is that the employees of the profitable division will pressure the deficient division to make a profit. If the deficient division does not start to turn a profit, the other employees and their division heads will pressure upper management to close that division.

In the end, teams that are able to play together, stay together. A company culture and system that rewards cooperation will produce employees who work across division lines to ensure long-term stability of the organization.

## Plan for Growth

Whether they are called marketing initiatives or strategic plans, all successful businesses rely on some form of conscious planning to lead them into the future. A simple definition of planning that people can understand and remember is: "Where does the future lie, and how do we position ourselves to generate a profit?"

In construction, that transfer is better when it's slow but sure rather than fast and furious. Many construction companies go out of business because of too much work, not too little.

Through leadership, plans guide employees into achieving measurable results in the area of customer retention and increased revenue and profit. They also guide the entire company about how this will be accomplished in terms of shared values and personal responsibility.

Plans that are developed without an initial reality check are a waste of time and money. The formulation of such faulty plans usually starts with an out-of-town executive retreat with an outside facilitator who has inadequate experience in the construction industry. Those facilitators present generic templates of objectives, strategies and tactics, and burden the participants to fill in the blanks. Many hours are consumed with deep thought, consternation and mixed feelings.

Eventually the walls in the meeting room are filled with large sheets of paper containing hundreds of bullet points, graphs, charts, mission statements, values statements, and so on.

After reaching the point of too much information, the road map of the new, theoretical, and untested plan is given the name Mountain. Your customers and prospective customers live on the top of that mountain. The road to the top is called Objective. To get to the objective, many side roads must be taken which are called Strategies and each strategy has many tasks called Tactics which must be accomplished before you can get to your Objective. The list of things to do formulated at the executive retreat could be in the hundreds.

Now back in town with your employees, you expect them to get on the bus with you to the top of the mountain. One big problem: nobody asked the employees before the retreat for any input. They may not have the motivation or proper attitude to get on the bus. Furthermore, they may have critical input about the business which has not been included in the plan because you didn't ask for it.

Typically, back at the office, the mountain of work to do and organizational changes to be made are first resisted and then completely ignored. People in the organization are granted the excuse that they are too busy doing urgent things. The plan is filed away to gather dust and the organization goes back to business as usual. Without employee buy-in, a plan will frustrate upper management and be viewed by employees as just another set of empty words.

Also back in town are your customers. Big problem number two: Nobody asked the customers what they want and need. This is why inventions like the suede raincoat, solar-powered flashlights and impact-activated parachutes end up in failure—nobody bothered to ask potentials customers if they would ever make a purchase.

On the other hand, inventions for the construction industry like gloves, hardhats, safety glasses, ladders and cordless tools remain successful because it is something that we want, need and are willing to purchase. I envision a scene where that bus is going up the mountain with windows rolled up, while on the side of the road are employees and customers shouting unheard statements at the bus such as "What about . . . You should consider . . . Have you thought about . . . Care about the . . . Keep in mind . . . We can . . . We won't . . . Will you . . ." and "We would like to." But unfortunately they were not listened to. What do your customers want and need and are your employees able to produce that?

> "The plan developed solo will likely have to be implemented solo."
>
> - Dean Korthof
>
> "Those convinced against their will are of the same opinion still."
>
> - Dale Carnegie

Another major problem with plans is they are strategic only for the time period in which nothing changes. In other words, your plan is applicable and current so long as your customers remain constant and your services remain in demand. However, when important changes occur, many plans become obsolete.

Years ago there was a successful general contractor who focused on building assembly plants for the automobile industry in Detroit, Michigan. The downturn in that market area rendered his plan obsolete. Likewise, many contractors had successful marketing plans to install asbestos insulation for fireproofing and insulation until it was banned. Thus the plan was only good for the time period in which nothing changed.

Therefore, your plan should be defined around what your employees are able to produce and what your customers are willing to purchase from you, all the while separating yourself from your competitor on some basis other than low price.

Other important things that affect plans include a sudden loss of your key marketing people, an unexpected drop in financing, changes in government regulations or political control, wars, natural disasters or a number of other unexpected changes that make you say: "Now what are we going to do to generate revenue?"

Another problem with some plans is they are too restrictive because they only take into account what is known at the time they are drafted. By design, these plans dismiss opportunities that do not fall into the narrow categories of market penetration. A marketing plan that restricts a company to a certain geographic area will dismiss an opportunity from a key customer to build their new project outside the region. Likewise, a restrictive strategic plan may dismiss an opportunity to take advantage of emerging markets that were not contemplated when the marketing plan was drafted. Emerging markets for contractors in the past have included the Interstate Highway System, manufacturing plants for warships and tanks, Silicon Valley, power plants, ethanol production and wind energy. Niche markets can also be great, provided competitors don't flood in and/or the demand doesn't dry up. Are you prepared to recognize the next opportunities and know if you should get involved?

Does your company need a plan? It depends. A plan is required if a new company is being developed, or if an existing company is going to expand into a new region or type of service. Creating a plan in those situations is productive because it forces those involved to determine the who, what, where, when, and how in order to prove to themselves and others (for example, board members or financiers) that the new initiative has a chance of success. Those efforts are much more effective than some plans which are no more than "Let's give it a try and see what happens."

I don't see a big need for a formal plan if a company is already established within their geographic location and has a constant group of customers in a steady or growing economy. Why spend the money telling each other what you already know? I would instead take that time and money and spend some face time entertaining those customers to further develop the relationship and realize what a jewel of a situation you have.

Common sense should guide your plan, whether it is formally written or just in your head. It should tell you, for example, not to bid on a nuclear power plant or offshore oil rig if you have no experience. Instead, common sense will tell you that this industry is risky enough without volunteering yourself to take on initiatives that present a high probability for failure. Use prudent judgment in evaluating your knowledge, experience and capabilities, and create a plan that maximizes your strengths and minimizes your weaknesses.

In summary, plan responsibly to a realistic goal. Don't believe that hope and chance make a strategy. Hope and chance offer encouragement in our personal lives during difficult times, but should not be the basis of a business plan. Instead, you must understand that effective planning starts with consensus, and is implemented through objectives and tactics that are mandated to be complete within timetables. Without the excitement of passion, the goals will lose energy and collect dust in a three ring binder or will get buried and forgotten in the word processor.

## Use Your Influence

Influence is your ability to produce positive effects upon another person's behavior. It's about using leverage and access in order to impact a situation. Influence is not neutral, however: it can be used in a good way to benefit, but also in a bad way to harm. It can be selfish or benevolent.

My first encounter with the use of influence was at the age of seven when we lived near a Dairy Queen which became a primary hangout. I knew the shop owner, who ran out of bananas for the banana splits during a busy day but did not have time to go to the nearby grocery store for more. He gave me a dollar and asked me to go to the store to buy some bananas.

Upon returning from the store, the DQ owner was disappointed because the bananas I delivered were soft and turning brown. I told him all the bananas looked that way. He then asked that I return to the store and tell the manager the bananas are for the DQ.

When I returned, the store manager said, "Why didn't you tell me that in the first place?" Then he went to the back room and gave me a group of fresh bananas that were firm and bright yellow with a slight tint of green. When I got back to the DQ, the owner said, "Now that's more like it." I thought this was unfair by idealistically thinking everybody should have equal and fair access to the best of everything, including bananas. It also made me realize the power of influence.

The Preamble to the U.S. Constitution says: "We the People of the United States, in order to form a more perfect union, establish justice, insure domestic tranquility, provide for the common defense, promote the general welfare, and secure the blessings of liberty to ourselves and our posterity." The Declaration of Independence lists the three aspects among the unalienable sovereign rights as "life, liberty, and the pursuit of happiness."

Neither of those documents mentions anything about life being fair.

Using unfair influence such as bribery or kickbacks to get your next project is not what I am suggesting, but I do suggest you use your influence in a positive way to benefit your company. Using your influence is what gets you a preferred reservation time and better table at your favorite restaurant while others wait. That may seem unfair but it is also a fact of life. It also seems unfair when you are the low bidder, yet do not get the contract because your competitor used his influence over you and with the customer. That successful use of influence to get the award of the next contract stems not from ill-placed demands but instead from a tangible and timely request for the return of a legitimate and valuable favor.

The very definition of an award is to give something to someone to recognize excellence. In construction, the use of influence to get the next contract is to be rewarded for past excellence and recognition of superior performance. Influential excellence for leaders in construction includes being on the board of directors at private universities and raising money for the next construction project. It's also convincing the customer that your company is truly the only one that has the experience and capacity to perform the work. That influence is about taking advantage of your earned distinction.

## Prepare for Failure

Professional boxer Mike Tyson has been quoted as saying: "Everybody's got a plan until they get hit." Imagine receiving a call from the job site telling you that a gang box on an upper floor fell through a temporary grating and landed on top of someone. You must have a disaster triage system organized and practiced prior to emergency incidents.

Where I live, there was a construction-related accident involving a fire that lasted just fifteen seconds, yet caused serious injuries. The following morning the newspaper had already investigated and reported the status of injuries and where they were treated. They had also reported the name of the employer and the number of times it had been investigated by OSHA, the Health Department, the Pollution Control Agency and the Department of Labor and Industry. The article also included various opinions from people that were incriminating against the company. Be assured that, with a major incident, the media will get involved and in your face.

Unfortunately some accidents can't be prevented, but with advance planning you can prevent a public relations disaster for your company. Responsibilities to be delegated include: who is responsible for reception of calls to the office; who is going to the job site to assure the avoidance of further danger; who will contact family members in the event of serious injury or death; who drafts the written statements and conducts the interviews with the media; and who contacts the customer to advise of the ongoing status of the emergency and the job.

You can't afford for a serious accident to happen before you figure out what to do. There are consulting companies that specialize in crisis management that can provide services for your preparation and practice. It involves the assignments of who does what in an emergency situation including role playing in simulated mock emergencies. The anxiety and stress you will feel just in the simulation will provide an understanding of the great importance of this responsibility.

## Ease Pressure and Stress

I describe stress as being responsible for something, yet not having total control over the outcome. Farmers undergo stress because they are responsible for a crop, yet have no control over the weather. Contractors have constant stress to maintain a certain volume of revenue, yet have no control of their competitor's activity or some of the decisions of their customers. Contractors have constant stress to complete the work within budget and schedule, yet do not have control of other contractors on site or the weather. Burnout comes fast in companies where management induces pressure to work at maximum levels all the time, while raising expectations of job responsibilities and results.

All work and no play is exhausting and upsets balance. It fosters a culture where employees are pitted against each other in competition for who can work the most hours at the expense of their personal lives. Hard work gets confused with results where employees exhaust themselves for the sake of work but are unable to produce results.

Eventually they burst out with loss of motivation and concentration and find it hard to cope with irritability and mood swings. The three most stressful construction projects I have been involved with resulted in one project manager being taken off the job site in a straitjacket and two project managers committing suicide.

The most effective steps to reduce workplace stress are letting the employees know you care. Caring can include flexible work hours, on-site chair massage, a quiet room where employees can go and make private phone calls, recognition, surprise bonuses, or gifts.

I once noticed that an important project manager was dragging himself to work. High work stress was affecting his personal and work life. I surprised him with a plane ticket for him and his wife to go to Las Vegas for a long weekend, with the hotel also paid for by the company. He returned with a stress-free smile and the motivation to get back to work. It wasn't according to company policy, but it was still the right thing to do. Stress itself is not always a bad thing: instead, stress can be a self-induced motivator and a passion to achieve a goal.

**Henry Kaiser (1882-1967)**
Kaiser worked hard with enthusiasm which garnered customer and employee loyalty. For fifty years his company was successful in construction, shipbuilding metals, auto production, and real estate. He did not fear risk and was an opportunist. His mantra was, "Find a need and fill it."

**Thomas Edison (1847- 1931)**
Edison was very curious, competitive and hard working. Notable among his many inventions was the incandescent lamp. Being an opportunist, he became the first known contractor to provide single-source services for engineering, procurement and construction on a turn-key basis. He formed a company to install his lamps in many cities, and called it the Thomas A. Edison Construction Department.

**Peter McGuire (1852-1906)**
Demonstrating respect for the individual and fairness, McGuire had a passion for elevating the wages and working conditions for craft labor. He initiated the idea that local unions form into national unions to better protect their members, including the fight for an eight-hour workday. Peter proposed the idea of a holiday to give workers a day off. Twelve years later, Labor Day became a national holiday.

**Mort Mortenson Jr. (1936- )**
"We have a belief that there is something positive to be gained from everything we do. It lies in our capacity to look for the positive lessons in all circumstances. To be effective leaders, we must act with honesty and integrity. This means acting in such a manner that people will trust you to handle any matter in their best interest. Success is not often granted without experiencing the agony of tough times. It takes fortitude and character."

# Chapter Four

# The Subcontractor

The current relationship between general contractors and subcontractors did not always exist. In fact it is a relatively new arrangement in the relationship. Back in the days of building the pyramids in Egypt and for about 5,000 years afterward, construction activity was performed by the *architekton* (Greek) or *architectus* (Latin). Both words mean "master builder." They were trained in all aspects of construction and responsible for all phases of a project, including concept, design and construction. The master builder worked together with the owner without a general contractor because, in those eras, design was not separated from construction.

This method continued up until the eighteenth-century Renaissance period, when Michelangelo and other artists who did not have the training or ability to oversee construction began designing buildings. Instead of overseeing the entire process, they became the architect who created the design, but they were not directly responsible for the construction.

In this way, the role of the *architectus* evolved into the function we know today as an architect—someone who is primarily focused on the way the building affects the senses. The architect designs how the building looks and feels, by using various shapes, colors and materials to create the intended environment for their customer.

The other responsibilities of the original *architectus* have been assumed by the engineer and the general contractor. The engineer focuses on how the building supports itself, as well as how the building works. Then, in nineteenth-century England a new profession evolved known as "the general contractor." Today, the general contractor focuses on constructing the design of the architect and engineer with emphasis on adherence to budget, safety, quality and schedule.

From the beginning, general contractors have awarded contracts for specialized portions of their work to subcontractors. Subcontractors have niche talents and unique capabilities. They provide specialty construction services that general contractors are either unwilling or unable to perform, and thus allow the general contractors to transfer risk and reduce cost. Today subcontractors perform about seventy percent of the total construction in the U.S.

Even though subcontractors by definition are *sub*servient to the general contractor, they are also an undeniable influence, both positive and negative, upon the general contractor's success. Some general contractors are willing to admit this and others are not. For this reason, there is enormous inconsistency in the way general contractors and subcontractors consider and behave toward one another. Some regard one another as necessary evils and expect to fight through the project. Others regard one another as personal friends, or at least professional allies, and expect to provide mutual support for a successful project. Others are somewhere in between, depending on the level of either conflicting or harmonious moods, attitudes and personalities. More information about the psychology of the general contractor is discussed later in this book.

As a supervisory training instructor for the Associated General Contractors Association, I taught a course titled "Dynamics Between General Contractors and Subcontractors" in St. Paul, Minnesota. All the attendees were employed by general contractors and held job site supervisory positions.

At the beginning of the first class I asked the students to provide one word definitions of the word "subcontractor." Positive responses included: cooperative, team player, honest, safe, high quality, on time, smart, thinking ahead, problem solver, and friend. Negative responses included: lazy, unsafe, whiner, always late, excessive punch list of work to be redone, unreliable, arrogant, finger pointer, and liar as well as a whole host of other unsavory terms that I won't mention here.

All the attendees were convinced their perceptions were correct and they responded accordingly at the job site. For some reason, those who were more optimistic about their relationships with their subcontractors tended to have more successful projects and those who were pessimistic tended to have less successful projects.

Throughout my career, I've had the opportunity to ask the owners of several general contracting companies about their opinion of subcontractors. Their responses ran the gamut between very good and very bad. One general contractor said about subcontractors: "We are proud of the many things we do here with our subcontractors. We take care of them and they take care of us. We present none of our problems to the customer. We are very proud about receiving the Outstanding General Contractor Award from the American Subcontractors Association. That award means a lot to us and we worked hard to earn it because it's based on great execution of well-run projects, the practice of safety, fair treatment, and timely awards of contracts and payments."

Another general contractor said: "Subs are just necessary evils. We do all the legwork in preconstruction and they come in at the last minute and want a big profit. They have it easy; all they have to do is bid the work on the plans and specifications that we give them. Then when something goes wrong on the job site they whine and ask us to fix all the problems. I wish they would work as hard as we do."

In talking to subcontractors about their experience with general contractors, I've heard the same wide range of opinions. One subcontractor said of general contractors: "General contractors are my lifeblood because all my work comes from them. I would be out of business without them. I give them the respect they deserve, and I'm thankful for the opportunities they provide and the support they give me. I would be lost without them. Plus two of the general contractors I work with most are my fishing buddies."

Another subcontractor said: "I really like the construction business because you get paid to fight! I don't get this part about being nice, because you got to get them before they get you! Generals intentionally create a wall between us and the customer. They take credit for our job well done and in the meantime hold up payment on our invoices. They are a pain."

I remain amazed after forty-five years in the construction business that the brick and mortar remains the same, but the relationships are extremely different. Some prefer putting their best foot forward while others seem to prefer getting started on the wrong foot. I have been burned many times in this business. I have lost millions of dollars. I have been betrayed by those I mistakenly believed were honest business partners and customers. Regardless, I still insist on putting my best foot forward, choosing optimism about the next relationship instead of pessimism. In my experience, optimism is rewarded most of the time. When I start a job with the intention of working productively with business partners like subcontractors, it almost always goes well.

It is true that general contractors award to subcontractors, but it is also true that subcontractors can dictate which general contractor gets the job. On bid day, subcontractors have flexibility in pricing and can modify their pricing up or down to send a message to the general contractor for previous behavior. Subcontractors may be fierce competitors among themselves, but together they stay away from those general contractors who impose undue harm. Overall, it is the general contractor, not the subcontractor, who guides the direction for the success or failure of the project.

Let me tell you a true story to illustrate the importance of treating subcontractors fairly. There was a large general contractor who had several specialty divisions including highway/heavy, petrochemical and power production. The division managers often complained about the high cost of overhead that was allocated to their divisions for accounting services. To offset the complaints, senior management decided to convert the accounting department from an overhead cost to a profit center. In doing so, the accounting department strong-armed the low-bid subcontractors and forced them to lower their price by five percent as a condition of receiving contracts. Then they delayed the monthly progress payments by sixty days and delayed the ten percent retention payment by at least ninety days and placed that money into Certificates of Deposit.

The word spread throughout the subcontractors' associations and networks. Many of them refused to bid the general contractor and the ones who did increased their bid prices way above what they offered to their competitors. The delayed payments caused most subcontractors to call the general contractor's customers and demand that joint checks be issued for monthly progress payments. Many of the subcontractors also placed liens on the project every month which caused great inconvenience, irritation and nervousness in the customers.

To avoid the hassles, many of their customers instead invited the general contractor's competitors to bid on future projects. The customers knew the competition got along better with the subcontractors, because working with them did not require the hassle of joint checks and lien waivers. Eventually the general contractor's reputation was ruined and the customers continued to proceed on other projects without them.

The lesson the subcontractors delivered to that general contractor was: "Fool me once, shame on you. Fool me twice, shame on me." The lesson the general contractor learned—and the one I hope you will take away from this story—was: "Short-term profit comes at the high cost of long-term reputation and revenue."

Good general contractors are willing to negotiate fair contract terms and don't play win-lose games with their subcontractors. Good general contractors seek the right price, not just the super-low price, because relationships grow bitter soon after the sweet taste of the super-low bid goes sour. Superintendents from general contractors who enjoy good relationships with subcontractors say things like:

- "Subs are essential for our success and we feel comfortable in relying on each other for reliability and honesty."

- "We all work together to make the customer happy. This leads to the next project because a team that plays together stays together."

- "I know that mistakes will be made on both sides but that doesn't mean we have to hammer each other. I need honesty for both the good and bad news."

Realize that your customers view your subcontractors as a reflection of your ability to manage. When a subcontractor does something good or bad, it will be a direct reflection upon you, because your customers assume you control them. If your subcontractor completes a critical part of the work ahead of schedule, you will get the credit. Likewise you will receive the blame if the subcontractor is behind schedule. Subcontractors therefore have the same ability as you to either increase or decrease your reputation. It's similar to having a dog: if it performs well you get the credit, but you also get the blame if it misbehaves.

Here is another story about dealing with subcontractors: Our company was involved on a $110 million design-build project that on paper had little chance for success but ended with great success. It involved building two tunnels—each nineteen feet in diameter and 7,300 foot long—for a light rail train under a major international airport. The process utilized a "cut and cover" construction method at each end and a boring machine to cut the tubes under two runways as deep as seventy feet underground while the airport was in operation.

The schedule was aggressive and demanding. Some portions of work included penalties up to $25,000 per day for not meeting a milestone date which required some bidders to include three eight-hour shifts per day. This project did not start out great and included serious concerns from state legislators about cost and security. The low bidder was not awarded the project and filed a federal suit over the Airport Commission's decision to award to another bidder due to alleged violation of bidding rules.

When contracts were awarded, it created more potential for failure because the general contractor was a new joint venture headed by a construction company from another country. Our company was one of ten major subcontractors they hired. This new team included contractors and major equipment suppliers from all over the world who all had no experience working together as a single team. Once work started, the soil conditions presented unsteady limestone, difficult glacial material and gaps of air, plus muck and water. It also involved tons of paperwork in dealing with the various city, state and federal agencies.

So why was this project successful? I believe it was because of fear of failure. Not the fear that would cause someone to not go forward, but the fear that if this group of subcontractors did not join forces with each other and the general contractor, all of us would have failed. No one wanted to be the weak link in the chain. The consequence for project failure trumped individual selfishness in looking out for other contractors' schedule demands and personal concerns. It reversed the traditional interpretation of fear of failure and transformed it into courage to succeed. We all knew failure might lie ahead, but were still trying to win.

One of our managers for the project said: "After we were awarded the project we were a bit uneasy about being the low bidder on a type of project we never performed before. When we mobilized to site we found other contractors equally concerned about the difficulty and uniqueness of the project. Success started when the general contractor put his arms around all of us and asked, 'What do you need?' and 'How can we help you?' Better yet, the general said, 'We are not here to threaten you by saying we are going to bury you if you don't keep up.' That instantly fueled a spirit of cooperation among everybody. The general contractor was willing to listen to us even if the subject was about some constructive criticism."

## Principles of Success in Dealing with Subcontractors

Treating subcontractors fairly and valuing their contributions to a project is key to the success of a general contractor. How do you know what business practices will accomplish this goal and set you on the path to success? The most important principle is akin to the Golden Rule. When considering a business practice that affects your subcontractors, ask yourself how you would react if another contractor subjected you to that practice. If it wouldn't sit well with you, that's an indication that you may be on the wrong track.

It's not possible to discuss all the potential business practices that will serve you well when working with subs, but these seven principles are key to having successful and productive relationships:

- Choose subcontractors wisely
- Evaluate bids
- Talk to all bidders before awarding the contract
- Never "bid shop"
- Ask for reasonable changes
- Offer appropriate support
- Pay on time

**Choose Subcontractors Wisely**

Many subcontractors may want to bid to you on a particular project, but you don't have to invite the whole world. This is especially true in a world where some subcontractors have your interest in mind and others have only their interest in mind. Decide if you want the right price or the super low price. Choose bidders who have the same values you do in terms of customer service, bidders who have a good reputation in the community, bidders you've worked with successfully in the past, bidders who have a cooperative attitude toward working with general contractors, and bidders with whom you can imagine being friends. You can buy sweet apples or sour lemons but don't fool yourself into thinking they are the same.

**Evaluate Bids**

Every contractor given enough time will eventually commit a major mistake in the calculation of their bid price. A super-high price can be dismissed but a super-low price, even though tempting, should not be accepted without verification of legitimacy. Alerting the subcontractor to his super-low price shows great respect. It also may avoid the subcontractor from pulling his bid after you have committed to it, leaving you with a major void in that bid amount and the much higher price of the second place bid. It can also help you avoid having to tell your customer that your subcontractor went broke halfway through the job.

The resolution to this problem on bid day is very simple. Just pick up the phone and call the senior person responsible for that bid proposal and say something like this: "We have received your bid proposal. We are not going to share your competitors' bid prices, but it is obvious that your bid amount is significantly lower than your competitors. We are concerned and request that you review your proposal." This simple act is not only ethical and moral, it may also save a disaster for both of you while enhancing your reputation for fairness.

## Talk to All Bidders Before Awarding

When requesting value-based proposals that measure not only price but also experience and team strength, you need to talk to all of the subcontractors you invited and who submitted a proposal before awarding the contract. Have empathy for your subcontractors who spend many hours and much money in preparing those proposals just as you do. Awarding without having a meaningful and honest conversation with all the bidders makes the unsuccessful subcontractor wonder if your mind was already made up before you sent out the request for proposal.

Conversations should include a scope of work review to determine an apples-to-apples comparison of all bidders' proposals. It should include an evaluation of value engineering items authored by the subcontractor that could either reduce cost or enhance the existing design. Also consider qualified labor availability and the project manager's degree of project experience and personal excellence. Going through this process ensures that the unsuccessful bidders at least feel their effort was worthwhile. It shows them that it was the weakness in their proposal that caused them not to get the job rather than thinking that you barred them from the job. This effort will motivate the subcontractor to bid to you in the future knowing that open communication and fair play are the rules of your game.

**Never Bid Shop**
"Bid shopping" is the unethical act of divulging the low price of one subcontractor to another in order for the competitor to reduce its price to become the low bidder. If you get caught at this, you should pack your bags and change your name, because you will never receive a legitimate bid price again. Your action will be spread around town and your reputation will be ruined. Just don't do it.

**Ask for Reasonable Changes**
Anyone who knows construction should not be surprised about changes in scope of work, schedules, weather and people. Change is constant but what isn't constant is the way changes are communicated to your subcontractor.

Do you give timely notice so the change can be accommodated with efficiency and lack of drama? Or do you call late on Friday afternoon demanding that several changes be made first thing on Monday morning?

Yes, there are exceptions for last minute unsuspected modifications but subcontractors grow tired real fast when contractors "cry wolf" and make exaggerated requests. In addition, a blooper on your part should not constitute an emergency on the part of the subcontractor.

**Offer Appropriate Support**
Disputes will always be part of construction. Sometimes the subcontractor is right and you (or the customer) are wrong. When that happens, come clean and support them in their legitimate request for extra time and money. The road to project success is two-way, not one-way.

**Pay on Time**
Fast pay equals fast friends. Subcontractors should not be expected to finance the general contractor's portion of the project through intentionally-delayed payments. If you expect them to perform on time they should be able to expect that you will pay them on time.

## Why and How to Terminate a Subcontractor

The construction industry is prone to conflict due to all the pressure to adhere to budget, safety, quality and schedule within an environment that is often plagued with interference and conflicting priorities. Therefore, be tolerant of your subcontractors who are making the good effort with the right attitude, even when—like all human beings—they make honest mistakes.

On the other hand don't be afraid to distance yourself from professional troublemakers. Some subcontractors are unwilling to take orders or adhere to the terms of the subcontract because they believe the rules are unfair. They will attempt to disrupt the project and seek out the negative with the preference for finger pointing over personal responsibility. Some people just can't get along and instead enjoy the challenge of a fight through fostering a development of adversity.

These types of people usually have a chip on their shoulder and think they are smart enough to wiggle around legitimate contractual obligations in the scope of their work. They also try to take advantage of imprecise contract language by converting requirements into illegitimate change order requests, even though the costs were already included in the original bid.

Subcontractors like this also like to point out the errors of others yet are unwilling to provide positive direction. They are dramatic while drawing a line in the sand and operate within an alienated position while attempting to exercise power in addition to making endless demands of your time. The best thing to do is cut your losses by removing them from the job site . . . even if you're a nice guy.

The following red flags should be viewed as "failure ahead" signs for your relationship with a subcontractor:

- Asking questions about the procedures for arbitration and litigation at a pre-bid meeting
- Submitting a super-low bid price
- Being unable to provide a performance or payment bond
- Submitting a scope letter after the bid date instead of before

- Making nickel-and-dime change order requests for all the small and low cost changes
- Saying "We forgot to include this," or "We were told not to include this," as a reason for large change order amounts.
- A pattern of broken promises on schedule and other commitments
- Taking shortcuts on quality, such as unauthorized installation of substandard materials and equipment
- Disregarding the safety of their employees and of others
- Presenting fabricated or forged lien waivers from their subcontractors
- Whining and complaining to your customer about your performance
- Repeated turnover of their key personnel in both office and field

When you begin to see these red flags with your subcontractors, above all, do not try to convince yourself that things will get better. Stripes on zebras do not change, and the bite of a stingray is always painful and dangerous. Instead, remember Albert Einstein's definition of insane: doing the same thing over and over again and expecting different results.

Unfortunately for bad subcontractors, general contractors have the power of the pen in writing and enforcing onerous contract language. With one click on their computer keyboard they can withhold payments.

When it comes time for the termination, make it swift and sure. Swift in that you will accept no more excuses, because you no longer expect that their required performance will be achieved. Swiftness will also protect you from the embarrassment of having your customer beat you to the punch and demand their removal from the job site.

The termination also needs to be sure. You must have sure documentation about the subcontractor's failings and responsibilities. In addition, your actions must be supported by your contract language, including the provisions under failure to perform and breach of contract.

This is a serious legal act. You will want to work with your attorney to help protect you against possible counter claims by the subcontractors including unjust termination for failure to coordinate the work, failure to make progress payments, and loss of anticipated profits. In fact, terminating a contract without the subcontractor defaulting on a substantial (material) contract provision could backfire and result in a breach of contract on your part. Preparations with your attorney will include notification to the surety providing the subcontractor's performance bond, selecting a replacement subcontractor, and notification to your customer regarding the intended termination. You should also have a solid plan to reduce the disruption of work that will be caused by the demobilization of the terminated subcontractors plus the mobilization and learning curve of the replacement subcontractor.

Back in the nineties our company was involved in a critical addition to a water treatment plant for a city with a population of 60,000 people. We hired just such a subcontractor to install a new water main pipe system which then had to be connected into the existing pipe system thirty feet underground. When completed, the new system would service the city's drinking water and fire hydrants. During the course of construction and prior to the important pipe connection, the owner of the subcontracting firm broke many promises about meeting schedule milestones, had unfounded excuses as to why he could not perform his work, and submitted several illegitimate change orders.

I refused to authorize payment for the change orders because it was obvious in reading his scope letter and contract that the cost of the work was clearly included in his base contract price. He responded by threatening me, "I will get even with you someday!"

That day came at the critical point of the project involving the connection of the existing piping system into the new one. That required the shutdown of the water system where hundreds of the homes and fire hydrants were without water pressure. The fire chief and city inspector were present on the job site and anxiously waiting for restored water service. The subcontractor only had one hour to make the connection.

Instead of making the pipe connection, he drove his crane thirty feet down the ditch and blocked the access. He turned the engine off and walked away and instructed his crew to sit and do nothing. He approached me, saying, "I have some new change orders that I would like to discuss and get a promise of payment from you before I make the pipe connection."

I told him: "Your change orders are phony and this was not the time to talk about them. Get back in the ditch and make the pipe connection. You are wasting the little time we have!" He poked me in the chest with his fist, at which point the fire chief called the police, who arrived in three squad cars and with dogs barking. I told the subcontractor, "You are in breach of contract by not making the connection."

He replied with his attempted power play by saying, "I know I am, but the contract I signed with you allows me three days to remedy the breach. You don't have three days to make this connection. You only have what is left of the one hour!"

I said, "With all you have done and have not done, you have been in breach of contract for months. Go down and make that connection, or I will."

He replied, "I'm not going to and you aren't either."

I turned away from him and saw the city inspector, fire chief, and police officers looking at me as if to say, "What are you going to do?" I gathered our employees working on the job site, and told them, "If he doesn't start to work in making that connection in five minutes, then get your cutting torches out and cut his crane apart. Then use our crane to lift his out of the ditch. Then we'll go ahead and make the connection ourselves."

Looking nervously at the subcontractor, our foreman asked me, "Are you serious?"

I answered, "Very serious."

Moments later, the subcontractor surrendered his fight and

completed the pipe connection. The following day I terminated his contract and removed him from the bidders' list for future projects. He continued his bad behavior with other contractors—and went out of business a few years later, because contractors refused to invite him to bid or would not accept his bid no matter what the price was.

The story at the beginning of the chapter showed the power that subcontractors have to harm general contractors who treat them unfairly. This story shows the power of general contractors over the livelihood of subcontractors who misbehave. The important lesson in both cases is that general contractors and subcontractors are mutually dependent. Treating subcontractors with respect, and expecting the same in return, is the path to success as a general contractor.

At this point in the book I reflect on a person I have known and respected for over thirty years. His name is Dean Korthof and his careers have spanned the role of being a subcontractor, general contractor and a customer for both. His wisdom enlightens and provides good sense to others. His assessments about personal and work life are remarkable. His distinguished quotes are simple to understand, yet were born from complicated experiences.

### On Success:
"Trust is the only real thing we have to sell."
"Trust and respect: like any worthwhile crop, they must be nurtured and tended."

### Between Success and Failure
"You have to determine who is fact and who is fiction."

### On Failure:
"We need to have better learning curves than mistakes."
"Making excuses is a good way of making ex-customers."

This last quote gets back to the saying expressed in Chapter 2: "People do business with people they want to do business with. Somehow they find a way. The trick is to find that way." Dean found that way by being smart about his job and good with people. So can you.

> "Success is created through partnerships, effective communication, trust, honesty, reputable subcontractors and timely payments. Failure is caused by adversarial relationships, inexperienced subcontractors, lack of communication and trust, excessive change orders and slow payments."
>
> > - Bruce Quam, President,
> > DJ Kranz Construction Co.

Chapter Five

# Relationship Success

U p to this point in the book, my focus has been on success or failure on the levels of the overall industry and specific businesses. The next two chapters will focus on how the individuals within your company can create successful customer relationships and loyalty as well as the mistakes they make that cause relationships to end.

The first step in creating customer loyalty is to build relationships. Establishing relationships is a big challenge because it requires an investment of time and emotion for which there may not be any measurable results in the short-term. It also requires the initial period of one-way gain: in other words, you have to expect to do for your customers without expecting they will do for you. Not until the relationship is earned should you expect that the customer will do something special for you.

"Doing for them" includes taking a genuine interest in their personal life while also volunteering to provide budgets, constructability consulting, and all the things required to make their personal and business life better and easier. When you have been successful in smoothing the way for them, the customer will go out of their way to do for you—for example, negotiating the next project without any competition.

Once you have built relationships, you must maintain them. The job of creating the relationship doesn't end when you get the first contract, but continues throughout the working relationship, over decades. The quality of the relationship with your customer determines loyalty more than the price of your product. Loyalty occurs when you are first on the mind of the customer. At the time of need for the next construction project, the customer will think about the quality of the relationship first.

## Build Relationships

In previous chapters, I've discussed the company practices that build customer relationships. Now, let's talk about the individual relationships your employees can develop with customers. Company policies can support relationships, but in the end relationships come down to people.

The employees who are typically most involved with customers are business development and project managers. Depending on the organization and size and of the company, estimators, senior managers, and owners may also have significant relationships with customers. However, everyone who supports the sales effort—including receptionists, administrative staff, and safety—needs to know the game plan so they can match the guidelines when supporting those directly involved with the customer. Everyone in your organization should know that it is their responsibility to treat customers like people who are personally important to their colleagues, to the business, and ultimately to their paychecks.

Teach your employees eight guidelines to help them build positive relationships with customers. Make the guidelines public, so that all employees can learn from them. Let everyone know what you expect when it comes to building relationships with customers.

- Meet face to face
- Friendship first, business later
- Let them bring business up first
- Use the customer's name
- Be trustworthy
- Listen to the customer

• Support empathy
• Build rapport

## Meet Face to Face

Back in the old days when bytes came from mosquitoes and hardware was a type of store, account managers actually got in their vehicles and drove across town to have a nice chat with their customers. This physical exercise produced the friendship, trust, listening, empathy, and rapport which I believe is significantly restrained through electronic communication.

I do not mean to criticize the era of electronic communication. It is a great time saver and source of instant information and communication. On the other hand, it has created a void in personal relationships simply due to the lack of face-to-face encounters. Some psychologists are concerned about the growing obsession among people who would rather interact with their electronic devices than with other human beings. Some people are giving pet names to their devices and buying them outfits to wear. Others use them at social events to avoid eye contact and conversation. Such antisocial behavior makes it extra difficult, or not even possible, to develop important relationships. I am concerned that, for some people, the more they are connected to the digital world, the more they become isolated from the interpersonal world.

In her book *Stop Walking on Eggshells*, Randi Kreger writes, "As it turns out, all the techniques we memorize may matter less than our body language, which communicates a whopping ninety-three percent of our attitudes and beliefs about something."

If that is true, electronic communication allows for only about ten percent of transmitted communication to be interpreted. The nonverbal cues are left out, including body language and voice usage. Words are an attempt to limit and frame a thought and format it verbally.

Throughout our human history, body language and voice usage have been trusted more than the words we communicate. Even if we are unaware of it, body language and voice usage still influence most of what we take in when someone else is speaking. Without full (one-hundred percent) communication, the relationship will be stuck in the logical decision making mode described in Chapter Two, where the sole determining factor in buying construction services is the low bid. Many contractors who claim that the low bid is the only thing that matters would not recognize their customers if they sat next to them.

Yes, I know that face-to-face meetings take time out of a busy day. If you want your employees to meet face to face with customers, you have to allow for the extra time it takes to drive across town and fight for a parking spot. It helps to remind yourself that it is one thing you are doing that hopefully your competitor is not doing. Maybe someday the face-to-face encounter will be replaced with holograms, but for now hitting the road will have to do because it still makes a huge difference in maintaining customer relationships.

Another advantage of regular face-to-face encounters is saving the embarrassment when you finally visit with a customer after a long absence to discuss the big upcoming project. When you ask, "When did you change your hairstyle?" and the customer responds, "About a year ago!" you know that you're missing the face-to-face component of your business development. Such neglected face-to-face communication is an embarrassment to the employee and an insult to the customer.

## Friendship First, Business Later

Earlier in this book I stated my motto: "People do business with people they want to do business with and somehow they find a way. The key is finding the way." To help your customers want to do business with you, encourage your employees to use the two-step process of friendship first and business second. Business friendships start with shared values, common interest, fun, responsiveness, straight talk, respect, dependability, attitude, and social rapport. Those in turn lead to customer interest, comfort, trust, and eventual loyalty.

If you want your employees to prioritize friendships when working with customers, you'll need to support them even when their relationship-creating efforts might look like goofing off to other employees. One way to do this is to make sure from the get-go that all employees understand what you are asking your salespeople to do with customers and why it's important. Once you've done that, it is easier to remind employees why it is important for some of their colleagues to spend business time on what look like social commitments.

In my company, one employee whose job required him to be in the office all day had issues with one of our salesmen and complained to others. The complaints were either due to jealousy or lack of awareness about him not being in the office, when in fact a major part of his job was to visit with customers. One day he complained to me after he overheard a phone conversation. "It bothers me when John calls up his buddies during the workday and talks about golf, fishing, and dinner with spouses. He laughs and jokes while he spends company time talking about their personal lives."

I responded by saying: "He is doing his job. Those people he is talking to are our good customers and also his good friends. Those people he is talking to are the same ones we negotiate contracts with."

An important discipline required for the friendship to be genuine is for employees to maintain personal and business relationships on a regular basis. This is the discipline of "unconditional love," meaning you must love to be involved with your customer even during their slow times when they have few projects or no projects to be built. The nature of our business requires a lot of "talk time" for customers to warm up to their upcoming projects.

I have often heard customers complain that some general contractors only offer "conditional love"—meaning that they only hear from those contractors when a project has been announced. One project owner who was exposed to conditional love told me, "I am offended and feel taken advantage of by phony relationships. These general contractors ignore me when I don't have major projects on board, but then try to treat me like an old friend when I do announce a big project. It appears they don't want my friendship, just my money. It must be the same feeling for lottery winners who get phone calls from old friends and relatives they haven't heard from in years."

## Let the Customer Bring Up Business First

Another discipline in the initial stage of creating a customer relationship is to not talk about business until they do. Have you ever gone to an industry social event and some vendor or subcontractors approaches you and hounds you about what you are bidding on? Do you feel like you are in a deposition? Do you say to yourself: "Hey, I'm here to socialize, not talk business?" Remember that your customer may feel bothered by your employees in the same situation. If they want to talk business, they will let your people know.

For example, I had a boss who challenged me to establish a relationship with a large manufacturer whose growth rate indicated they would initiate new construction projects in the near future. Their manager of construction accepted my invitation to play golf. Although it was frustrating, I did not bring up the subject of their future business construction plans. Instead, I listened and responded to whatever the prospective customer wanted to talk about—and it did not include one word about construction. Instead we talked about the joy of playing golf, his daughter in college, and his hunting dogs.

The next day my boss grilled me about what types of projects they had pending and when we could bid them. I told him I did not know.

With disappointment he asked why. I told him the subject never came up.

He replied, "Why then did you waste a day of company time and expense?" I told him it was not a waste but rather an investment in the relationship. Eventually, the investment of that short amount of time paid off in over a decade of continuous construction projects.

When you send a salesperson to make a connection with a customer, don't put pressure on them to bring in business the next day. Instead, know that every mighty oak tree was once a little acorn and the relationships your employees are building can grow over generations.

## Use the Customer's Name

One of the sweetest sounds in the world is for someone to hear their name. This simple discipline of saying, "Hi, Mary, it's good to see you," is a genuine gesture as compared with "Hey there, what's happening?"

Teach your employees to remember and use your customers' names. Dale Carnegie, an American lecturer and developer in courses on salesmanship, said: "If you want to win friends, make it a point to remember them. If you remember my name, you pay me a subtle compliment; you indicate that I have made an impression on you. Remember my name and you add to my feeling of importance."

Addressing someone by their name requires the ability to remember someone's name. How many times have you noticed someone you know walking toward you, yet you have forgotten their name? This is especially uncomfortable when you are in a situation where you would be expected to introduce them to others around you.

You can teach your employees to use an easy and effective way to recall someone's name. It revolves around the common frustrating statement, "The name is on the tip of my tongue and I know if I don't think about it, the name will come to me." Then, as you drive home, the name pops into your head. The reason for this untimely recall is in the difference between your conscious mind and subconscious mind.

The conscious mind retains what we are thinking about at the moment. The subconscious mind retains things we are aware of but not thinking about at the moment. Things the subconscious level is retaining are available to be sent to the conscious level.

If the name you are trying to recall is not of major importance, or if the last recall was a long time ago, that name is probably stored in the subconscious mind where it will be stored forever barring some mental or physical disability. Think of the subconscious mind as a file clerk who has in its files the first and last names of every name that entered your conscious mind.

You can tap that subconscious level if you realize that it is one-hundred percent guaranteed that their first and last names will start with letters between A and Z. Play the mind game by thinking of each letter in the alphabet in turn, starting with A. Usually the name will pop up before you get to Z. Sometimes only the first letter of the name pops up, so then it's easy to determine the next letter by starting over at A. If the first letter is a vowel, try consonants for the second letter. If the first letter is a consonant, try both consonants and vowels.

There are other ways to remember customers' names and this is a place where a smartphone can actually help your employees out. They could take a photo to go with the entry in their electronic address book and then take a quick look before they head out to a networking or socializing event. They might be able to use LinkedIn or Facebook profiles as a way to review customers' names and faces ahead of time. With practice, employees can impress people by using a customer's name.

## Be Trustworthy

I believe that trust is probably the biggest human factor in the construction industry. Trust is the gateway to a successful relationship and getting the next contract. Trust is the ability to predict what other people will do and what situations will occur. It is a one-on-one engagement that allows the other person to take advantage of your vulnerabilities while expecting they will not. Help your employees understand how to be trustworthy in their customers' eyes.

Trust is a basic emotion described by the feeling of being safe with another person. In construction, trust is about establishing the project expectations when defining the goals and roles. Your customer builds expectations from your promises, but when the commitments are not met, the caustic emotion of betrayal may take over. As the construction industry is such a rough and tough, risk-taking environment, why are construction customers such emotional and sensitive people? It is because they give your employees trust and expect it in return. Inherent to the construction industry is the baring of souls and the requirement to expose oneself to the whims of unpredictability and change.

Where else other than the construction industry can you phone your customer and tell them that for a million dollars you will build them something at some future date, something that today is intangible? When they accept your offer they have volunteered to be vulnerable to you. They have purchased a gut feeling that at some future date your promises will be kept. They stand naked in hopes you will not betray their trust and take advantage of them.

The best way to support employees in their pursuit of a trusting relationship is to give them time. Help your employees understand that customers grant trust over time, as a result of having a series of interactions where they perceive that they are treated both fairly and well. Emphasize the importance of reputation—both of the individual and of the company—in doing business. Don't expect or tolerate acts of distrust like bid rigging and gouging the customer on change orders.

Teach your employees that trust may take a long time to build, but customers can identify untrustworthiness immediately. Customers notice evasive answers, lack of eye contact, and negative body language. For example, teach employees who may be nervous about interacting with customers how to say, "I don't know the answer to that, but let me find out," in a forthright manner instead of avoiding the question or making something up.

Also set high expectations for social involvement with the customer's family. Instead of just sending the customer a computer-generated birthday card, expect that they would get invited to the party and make sure they are on the "gift list."

To help your employees understand the extreme importance of trust, ask them to put themselves in the individual customer's shoes. Tell them to imagine that the customer just gave your company a large contract. The person who gave you the contract is approached by his boss and has the following conversation:

His boss asks, "What did you do today?"

Your customer says, "I awarded ABC Construction a large contract."

The boss asks, "Is it in writing?"

Your customer says, "No."

The boss asks, "Is there a completion date?"

Your customer says, "We are working on it."

The boss asks, "Is it a lump sum contract?"

Your customer says, "No, because the drawings are not complete."

The boss asks, "So are we exposed to change orders and extra work requests?"

Your customer says, "Maybe, yes."

The boss asks, "What do you mean, maybe yes?"

Your customer says, "Well, yes, we definitely are."

Help your employees notice how nervous your customer now feels about his relationship with his boss and how dependent his future success or failure is on your performance. Help them understand how much trust it takes for your customer to make that step. He can only do it if he can trust that you will not take advantage of his vulnerabilities.

One of the greatest compliments I received was during the negotiation of a construction contract involving a national food company. The food company acquired its competitor and decided to transfer hundreds of its employees to another state. They purchased a building which needed to be retrofitted within a very short period of time. When it came time to issue contracts, their senior project manager called me and said he did not have time to create drawing and bid specifications, nor go through the bidding process, because he needed to issue contracts ASAP. He told me he estimated our scope of work to be about $400,000 and asked if we could get started right away.

I replied, "Yes, but I'm curious how we got the contract with so little effort."

He replied, "I've known you long enough to be assured that I can trust you to help me build this project on time and in cooperation with the other contractors. I also believe that you will not take advantage of me or the company in your noncompetitive, cost-plus contract."

Maybe it was my calm demeanor and advice when he was panicked about the time constraints and lack of construction documents on his projects. Maybe it was taking the time to give him a good long listen when he talked about his philosophy on the meaning of life. Maybe he was testing my honesty when we were playing golf and my ball landed behind a tree. He asked if I was going to move it, and I replied: "No, that would be cheating." Maybe it was something else. The point is to instruct your employees that most any interaction with a customer, whether it is business or social, either builds trust or erodes it.

## Listen to Customers
Good listening skills require emotional strength and the temporary suspension of your agenda. It involves genuine patience, openness,

and the desire to understand. Listening is one of four forms of communication and it is intrinsically bound to speaking, reading, and writing. It is unfortunate that we are taught speaking, reading, and writing in school but not listening, so use this opportunity to practice your listening skills. Customers love to talk, so teach your employees to be quiet and listen. Help them learn to listen with the intent to understand, not respond. Have them give the person they are listening to the impression they are being influenced by what they are hearing. The idea is to foster an open and honest dialogue.

There is an old story of the salesperson that had a forty-five minute visit with his customer. During the entire meeting the customer did all the talking and the salesperson never said a word. At the end of the meeting, the customer stood up and shook his hand to congratulate him on receiving the order. The salesperson said: "Thank you, but what did I do to deserve the order?" The customer replied: "This was one of the best conversations I've ever had!" This is a funny story, but it hides a kernel of truth. Salespeople, who are stereotyped as being motormouths, are more apt to win contracts by listening than by talking.

To help them master this, the whole company needs to have a culture of respect and listening to the customer. Employees need to know that seeking to understand their customer requires the discipline of consideration and the courage to listen. You can practice the discipline of listening at your next employee group meeting.

Invite two of your employees to role play. Ask one to be the talker and the other to be the listener. Give them some innocuous topic to discuss, and tell them that the talker will talk first. The talker is given the talking stick (a piece of wood) to hold while he is talking. While the talker is talking about the topic, the listener's job is just that—to listen attentively.

When the talker is done, he gives the listener the talking stick. At this point, the listener must restate what he heard the talker say. The talker may correct the listener by asking for the talking stick back. The stick goes back and forth until both are convinced that the listener has understood what the talker said. This may sound easy, but trust me: it will take a few times back and forth to get it straight. Once the listener has fully understood what the talker said, they switch roles.

When the second talker is done, the second listener takes the stick and tells the talker what he understood, and the stick goes back and forth between them until they are both sure that the listener has completely understood the talker.

This may seem like a childish exercise, but effective communication is so important as to be a fundamental life or death situation. Think of the history of our human associations where world leaders, both political and religious, failed to communicate and started wars that resulted in many needless deaths.

I disagree with the saying "Sticks and stones may break my bones but words will never hurt me." Sometimes during conflict or disagreement, hurtful words are said, and courage is needed to take the high road and not react in the same hurtful manner. It also takes courage to not take the hurtful words personally but instead minimize the attacker, not yourself. Remember that two wrongs don't make a right—just because your attacker jumped into the sewer doesn't mean you have to jump in as well.

On the other hand, courage in listening is required when you've got it coming to you and someone you admire says, "We have to talk." Then have the courage to take it like a man and appreciate that it takes a good friend to be straight up and honest with you. Courageous listening is a major key to conflict management. Take the time to help your people learn to listen to one another and to your customers.

### Empathy

Empathy is having the ability and the desire to share the feelings, thoughts and emotions that someone else is experiencing. It's a trait that I believe not all people possess, but one that is required in order to understand and therefore support that other person.

Empathy is the opposite of narcissism. Narcissists are unwilling, and therefore unable, to establish genuine relationships. They are indifferent to the problems of others and uninterested in recognizing their feelings. They are about selfishness instead of selflessness and are more apt to compromise their values than to live them. They spend much time in the mirror absorbing esteem, admiration and affirmation instead of releasing sensitivity, sympathy and understanding. Their lack of empathy causes them to lack pity, and they feel no remorse after harming or offending someone.

In building positive relationships, empathy is a simple matter of collecting emotional information about the other person. The more you collect, the deeper the relationship. An unknown author wrote: "Friendship is a living thing that lasts only as long as it is nourished with kindness, empathy and understanding."

Empathy is a gift derived from what you have gone through in life. Most people have some ability to empathize with others, but I'm not sure that an employee can be taught empathy. You can determine those employees who have empathy and support that behavior toward customers. An employee who has high empathy has the ability and motivation to understand and adopt another person's viewpoint. They share the customer's emotions when something happens that affects both parties and desires to help others. They also don't have a problem shedding a tear over the announcement of bad news.

I have observed that people who lack empathy tend to be more self-centered and have no remorse for those they have hurt or concern for those who are hurting. They are also poor listeners who often don't have a problem interrupting when someone is talking.

In 1992, Italian scientists Pellegrino, Fadiga, Fogassi, Gallese, and Rizzolatti discovered a particular kind of brain cell called mirror neurons that cause us to mirror what other people do and are thought to be the basis of empathy. (They documented this discovery in *Experimental Brain Research* in an article titled, "Understanding Motor Events: a Neurophysiological Study.")

Mirror neurons are the reason people smile back at you or tear up when they see someone else crying. It is also why you protect yourself when you see someone get injured. Empathy lets you feel something in your body even though it really happened to someone else. It's putting yourself in your customer's shoes. If you have empathy, you can feel your customer's pain which will get you closer to resolving your customer's issues.

Supporting employees with high levels of empathy is key to entering the customer's door and keeping it open. A sale is defined as satisfying the customer's wants and needs. Empathy allows your employees to search those out and separate the two. It also allows employees to know when to back off if they sense the customer may be agitated or not in the best mood to talk at the moment. Empathy makes forging a very strong bond much easier. This results in greater trust by sharing personal thoughts, worries and doubts as well as proud achievements, dreams and goals.

## Build Rapport

You can build rapport by observing someone's actions and then responding back to them with positive affirmations. Rapport is bonding that is achieved by matching the other person's body language, looking them in the eye and nodding the way they nod. You can also teach employees to use statements such as "I hear what you're saying," or "I see your point of view," or "I know what you're going through." You know you have established rapport when your "talking" style has reached an amicable relationship with your customer's "listening" style.

There are eight guidelines for building rapport: meet face to face; friendship first, business later; let them bring business up first; use the customer's name; be trustworthy; listen to the customer; support them; and show empathy. These guidelines to building rapport are easy, require no special training and can be started today. They do, however, require a special discipline that may not be easy, and that is placing yourself in a subservient role with your customer. It requires the proactive acts of great courtesy, respect and nurturing while doing for them in anticipation of what they will eventually do for you. Be sure to keep your enthusiasm and eagerness for the next contract award but do it with patience and persistent staying power.

## Maintain Relationships

Relationships are like motorized vehicles. Once a car is built, it must be properly maintained or eventually it will wear out and stop working. It will need constant checking of fluid level and various pressures.

Likewise, maintaining a relationship requires the constant checking of your customers' level of expectancy, satisfaction, or frustration, and how much pressure that is putting on the relationship.

Remember that customers are also like teeth: if you ignore them they will go away. That lack of desire and activity to continue maintaining the relationship will result in the customer feeling there's complacency on the employee's part or the feeling that the good relationship is being taken for granted.

Here are some specific tasks and duties of employees to assure the relationship is being maintained effectively. Employees must be certain these are part of the company culture and a condition for keeping their jobs. This mindset requires extra effort and self-confidence. The employee will likely need continuous training and development so they are willing and able to react in these ways. In addition to constant business and personal contacts through phone calls, emails and social contacts, employees must develop these core skills:

- Solve problems
- Act on complaints
- Keep promises
- Go the extra mile
- When they don't know, don't guess
- Negotiate disagreements
- Return phone calls and messages
- Ask for their time
- Close out projects

**Solve Problems**

Problem solvers enjoy high job security. Why? Because your customers rely on them to make their lives easier. A common complaint from customers about contractors is that they are part of the problem and not part of the solution. Too many contractors expect the customer to hold their hand and solve their problems. Realize that your customers have their own problems and do not want to spend their time and energy solving yours or those of your subcontractors.

Problem solvers look for answers, not mistakes, and have the discipline and staying power to realize problems are inherent challenges and opportunities in the construction industry. They realize problem solving is not just about investigating and reporting but it takes the extra effort to present solutions and carry them out to completion. They do this willingly because they know that problem solving will be a major award criterion for the next project. It's a personal investment in themselves, and the payout is subconscious reliance from their customers. It is the subconscious state of the customer's mind that is telling his conscious level through sixth sense and gut feeling that his problems will be solved if he calls that person.

Problem solving creates extreme personal loyalty that trumps the company logo on your employee's paycheck. The problem solvers are the employees who take your customers along with them when they leave your company to go to work for your competitor. Realize that if the customer thinks he is having a problem, then it is a problem. When the customer has a problem, you have a problem. You must be first in their mind when it comes time for solving—if you aren't, then your competitor will be.

I recall a young project manager who complained to me in great frustration about his inability to get things done on his checklist. I asked what was stopping him. He replied that customers kept getting in his way because they were calling and wanting him to solve their problems. He seemed surprised when I told him that receiving such calls is a compliment to him. I told him he was elevated to a problem solver, which should be his highest priority. I asked him what would be the importance of a project manager position if there were no problems to solve.

To put it another way, if all the problems were solved by someone else, what would be the importance of your job? You must be with the customer for both the good times and, more importantly, for the bad times. During both times you have the freedom and responsibility to make decisions in their best interest. In return they will pay you an amount that is in your best interest.

After this conversation, this young project manager approached problem solving as a position of honor rather than an irritating intrusion. Twenty-five years later I consider that project manger the most successful in terms of customer loyalty and respect. When your customer is deciding who to invite to his next project he will think: I know there will be problems on this project—so who can I rely on most to solve those problems?

## Act on Complaints

Sir Colin Marshall once said, "The customer doesn't expect everything will go right all the time. The big test is what you do when things go wrong."

Overmanage customer complaints and make them an immediate priority. Be an overachiever to the point your customer says, "Wow, I didn't expect you to go that far in handling my complaint." The ability to transform upset customers into loyal customers is a cornerstone of long-term success. Surprises are inherent in the construction industry because every project built has never been rehearsed and things hit the fan. Companies that succeed in customer relationship management have a culture that is open to customer complaints and make it easy for employees to resolve customer issues. It's a philosophy of over-the-top activity to gain resolution.

The same positive attitude about problem solving is required for receiving complaints. When a customer calls you personally to complain, it should be received as a compliment to your relationship. As strange as it may sound, customers who give you their complaints are actually giving you a chance to keep their business. A complaint should be viewed as an opportunity to further solidify your relationship. Handling complaints should involve upper-management personnel who provide the customer with up-to-the-minute updates.

It's fun when things are going great with no complaints. It's also a time when you may not be able to separate yourself from the competition—that separation comes when complaints start. Do you separate yourself by pointing fingers and refusing to return calls? Or do you jump forward into the complaint knowing your ability to get the next job may hinge on your go/no-go decision?

We all make mistakes, so when it happens it's best to come clean, accept responsibility for personal failure and apologize. Demonstrate how you want to put things back as they were and offer compensation. Small mistakes can actually help. If you fail in a relatively unimportant way and go overboard in the recovery, the message sent and received by your customer is: "You are so important to us even for the little things, and we will react even more on the bigger things." Done well, making mistakes can actually increase customer loyalty.

Just because some of your customers do not complain does not mean they are happy with you. Their silence may be their lack of confidence in your willingness or ability to respond. Or perhaps you ignored them or belittled their contention when responding to their last complaint. Regardless, they have probably fired you in their mind and you don't even know it. They will just let you fade away by somehow forgetting to place you on the next bid list and tell you it's too late when you find out.

I went through this slow death when we had a service contract at a refinery. In the office, we assumed things were going well because we heard no complaints from the customer. We assumed that no smoke meant no fire (a really bad assumption at a petroleum refinery). What we didn't know was that the customer had a slow burn going against our company because our on-site project manager was not attending to his needs, while telling us in the office that everything was just fine.

Each unresolved problem was not a big one, but the number of them grew and grew, joining together and increasing the customer's frustration exponentially. We had already been fired but were the last to know. The customer summoned us to his office and told us the stories of all the unresolved complaints. With hat in hand we promised to start resolving the complaints as soon as the meeting was over. He replied that it was too late. He had already hired our competitor to eliminate his need to complain to us. The only other issue in his mind was how soon we could demobilize the job site to make room for our competitor's trailer.

Realize that people tend to forgive mistakes of the mind, such as memory lapses, but are less willing to forgive mistakes of the heart, such as laziness or apathy. Realize that to repair the mistake may cost a lot of money, but that money might be the price to keep your customer. Initially, the question about who is right and who is wrong does not matter. Show empathy, apologize, atone and thank them for the complaint. Don't make excuses: they usually don't care why the problem occurred. They just want to know what you are going to do about it. Make decisions for what is in their best interest. Handling major complaints should involve upper management personnel who drop everything and mange the resolution minute by minute.

## Keep Your Promises

I had the honor one year to serve as chairman of the annual meeting for the Associated General Contractors. The keynote event was interviews of those we considered legends in our industry. They had personally started their general contracting companies with shovels, wrenches and wheelbarrows and their companies had grown into some of the largest in the nation. I asked them, what would you recommend to a project manager who wants long-term success? They all responded in the same theme:

- "Do what you say you will do and keep your promises."
- "Follow through on your commitments, because failure to follow through makes you the weak link in the chain."
- "Always do what you say you are going to do—if you do that, everything else should fall into place."

## Go the Extra Mile

It's a trend these days for some businesses to keep track of how much time a customer service rep spends on each call and then penalize them for spending too much time or reward them for getting through more calls per shift. This may look like sharp business, but it clearly works against long-term customer satisfaction in the construction industry which requires instead extra time and sometimes money to go the extra mile. It seems that many in customer service are also unwilling to go the extra mile if the problem can't be fixed on a computer. Give your staff permission to do what is needed to support your customers. It will be repaid by an enhanced relationship in the long run.

When we were having our kitchen remodeled, my wife picked out two hanging light fixtures from the website of a national home improvement store. When we called our local store to purchase the fixtures we were politely, yet uncaringly, told by the "service associate" that the items were not in stock and she did not know when they would be reordered. Thinking she satisfied that problem, she asked if she could be of any more service. I smiled into the phone and hung up.

Then I called their competitor, who also told me the fixtures were not in stock. Rather than conclude the call, she asked if I would please hold. She checked the national inventory and, eureka! She found the two fixtures 375 miles away in Grand Forks, North Dakota. She apologized again for my two-minute wait and asked if I would like to order them. I happily agreed, even though I had not yet asked her the price.

Then the customer service rep connected me to a floor supervisor at the Grand Forks store, by the name of Bill. He told me that, according to the computer, the fixtures were in stock, but asked me to remain on hold while he physically walked to the area. With joy, Bill told me the two fixtures were in his hand and asked if I would like to purchase them. Again I said yes—still without asking the price. Bill stayed on the phone with me, delivered the light fixtures to the checkout area and introduced me to the checkout person, Katie. She also apologized for my inconvenience. I corrected her. "I'm loving all this great service!" I said.

Katie asked if I wanted normal ground shipment or overnight. I asked for normal ground shipment and gave her my credit card number. I did two things after the purchase: first I thanked them for going the extra mile . . . all the way to Grand Forks. Second I asked what amount will show on my credit card.

Within the next few weeks we purchased over five thousand dollars worth of additional fixtures and appliances from that store to finish our kitchen project. We did not purchase anything more from the first store.

What is your customers' experience with your company? Do you allow your employees the freedom to bypass constraining policy and procedure to impress the customer or do you have bureaucracy that requires filling out a fire extinguisher requisition form when the building is on fire? The moral of this story is clear: set high standards and live up to them.

### When You Don't Know, Don't Guess

As a young assistant project manager I was working at a job site for the construction of two four-hundred-megawatt power plants. I was eager to impress others and wanted to be viewed as someone with decision making abilities and overall project knowledge. Unfortunately I did not possess those skills—but it did not stop me from acting that way. When an owner's representative would ask me if we were on schedule for the week I would say, "Yes, I'm sure we are." Actually I did not know if we were on schedule but did not want to look either stupid or unprepared. Eventually the people that needed right answers no longer asked me. In the end it cost the company money and bruised my reputation.

Much is at stake with all of the moving pieces that go into a construction project, and accurate information is vital for success. I have learned through mistakes that it is respectful and appreciated when you admit you don't know. If you don't know, the next step is to find the facts and present them to those who need them. They will learn to depend on your information, not ignore it.

Remind your employees that, in the construction business, "The more you know, the more you realize how little you know." Our industry is filled with unbounded changes. If someone thinks he knows it all, he is simply ignorant of all the things he doesn't know. Help them learn to manage the pressure for an immediate answer when they don't have one—and teach them to find out who does.

### Negotiate Disagreements

There are as many resolutions to a problem as there are people working toward a resolution. You can associate, negotiate, arbitrate and litigate. The easiest way is to have an open and honest rapport with someone so that when problems arise they can be settled objectively, without drama, in a win-win situation. This way of approaching conflict is based on the wise prediction that problems will occur. You therefore presume with your associate that you are just going to get through each problem as it arises and then prepare for the next problem.

Negotiating is about finding out what the other party needs and then giving it to them. It often requires both parties to give something up to the other party in order to get their own needs satisfied. Make a list of what you are willing to give away in order to get what you want but don't give anything away unless you get something in return.

Arbitration and mediation are the result of a failed negotiation, and typically result from hurt feelings, hard-headed egos, unwillingness to admit weakness and stubbornness. It takes more time and requires payment to a third party to convince you of your weakness, liabilities, and vulnerabilities. Thus, arbitration and mediation intimidate you into settlement by reducing your confidence that you will prevail in litigation.

Litigation is sometimes short for "scorched earth." This happens when you draw a line in the sand and your wounded ego, distressed heart, and inflamed emotions trump logic and reason. This win-lose stance is filled with negative emotions and motivation for retaliation.

Beyond litigation is assassination. You may think I am using this term figuratively, but once in my career I admit to being worried about a literal assassination.

While I was a young project manager, our company had a multi-million-dollar contract for the construction of two large power plants. The entire project had many stresses including a tight schedule, insufficient budget, poor labor availability, difficult quality requirements, long commutes, extensive work hours and arguments over ambiguous specifications. Our crews were working around the clock and the job site was tense. The stress was such that a friend who was a project manager for another company committed suicide. Other people made it public that they were concealing guns and knives to intimidate against the threat of being fired. The owner's representative, Bob, was stationed onsite and was responsible for the one-billion-dollar budget. My wife and I developed a friendly relationship with him and his wife, which included having dinner at each other's homes on occasion. Although I thought he acted weird sometimes, he was the customer, and I tried to make the best of our relationship.

I was working late at the job site one night and around 10:00 pm, I received a call from Bob, who invited me to his office for an urgent meeting. He asked me to reinstall some construction work that had previously been installed, approved, and paid. He told me the rework was required because one of his employees damaged the work.

I told him we could redo the work for sixty-five thousand dollars. He responded that he wanted it done for free. I told him that the damage was not our fault.

He said, "You don't understand me."

I said, "You don't understand me."

He said, "I have something that will change your mind."

He leaned back in his chair and opened his desk drawer. He pulled out a large pistol, leaned across the desk and pointed it at my forehead.

My mind raced with many thoughts: Is it loaded? Will he shoot me? Will I die? Why such a big deal over sixty-five thousand dollars? Is he crazy? What should I do?

I asked him if the gun was loaded.

He said, "I know if it is or not, but you don't."

I said, "Okay, Bob, I'm going to assume it's loaded. I am going to stand up and turn my back to you and walk out of the room. If you shoot me, it will be in the back." When I stood, I actually felt the hair on my body rise up. I turned around and walked out without being shot.

A few weeks later, doctors discovered that Bob had a brain tumor in his frontal lobe, the part of the brain that controls judgment. He was soon removed from the job site and admitted into a long-term care facility.

Lesson learned: Be careful about approaching people. Just because you are having a good day does not mean they are too. In that case, I think I would have preferred arbitration, or even litigation!

The final important thing to remember about problem solving in construction is the Other Golden Rule. This rule dictates that whoever has the gold (money) rules over the payment timing and amounts. The owners rule over the general contractor and the general contractors rule over their subcontractors who rule over their sub-subcontractors. The rules of the game are simple: if you want to get paid on time, listen and do what I say. Not playing by that Golden Rule results in excuses for not being paid for progress payments and retention payments.

When negotiating it is always good to bear in mind the wise words of Eleanor Roosevelt: "Never allow a person to tell you no who doesn't have the power to say yes."

### Return Calls and Messages

With electronic communication you can't hide from the sender. The sender knows the communication was sent and the receiver knows it as well. Prompt returns are viewed by the sender as a sign of respect and a confirmation that the sender has high priority and significance to the receiver. It also demonstrates a commitment to the relationship.

When replies to the sender are ignored or delayed, things can go bad in a hurry. People have a tendency to think the worst. It's similar to the worry reaction that parents have when their children are late and do not call. For parents, the worry stems from the duty to protect the child. Customers worry about their worth or value to you. An ignored or delayed reply can have the customer thinking "What's wrong? Why am I not getting a reply?" or "If I was respected I would have received a reply by now," or "There must be something much more important and a higher priority than me," or "I feel like I'm being left out in the cold."

Failure to promptly return phone calls, emails, or text messages is an ever-increasing cause of frustration for customers. They can transform a fragile self-esteem into a hardened heart because it is viewed as rude and disrespectful. With a continued pattern of abuse, the frustration evolves into feelings of contempt and dismissal for you and your company. I heard a customer describe why their existing contractor did not get the next job. He said: "Their project manager is smart and experienced but I don't want to work with him anymore because he doesn't return my calls as fast as I need."

The prompt return of calls and messages is an essential act in a successful business relationship. Likewise a delayed response, or worse yet, no response at all, is an essential act in the destruction of a relationship. It separates the respected from the disrespected, the timely from the ill-timed and the mannered from the ill-mannered.

A delayed response can be costly as well to job site productivity. There is little or no justification for a lack of response in this day of lightning speed communication. Employees should be expected to communicate ASAP with customers as an important part of their job description. Communications should be used as a criterion during performance reviews.

While on the subject of phones, I suggest what the president of a construction company does. Every morning he creates a new greeting on his voice message with something like: "Hello, this is Bill. Today is Monday, May 14th. I will be in a meeting from 9:00 am until 10:00 am and then again from 1:30 until 2:15. Please leave a message." This quick, easy and unique style of communication gives the listener the impression that Bill is engaged and informed every day, in control of his schedule and respectful of other people's time.

## Ask for Their Time

How many times have you received a phone call while you are pressed for time or focused on something important? The phone rings, you answer, and a salesperson rambles on about what he can sell to you or talks about some minor thing you have no time to listen to. You sit there half-listening while regretting ever picking up the phone call. The same thing can happen when your employees are calling your customers. If it's a bad time, your company's calls will be deemed an irritant, and the irritation will grow the longer the conversation lasts.

When they are calling your customers, train your staff to consider that it may be a bad time to call, and to ask customers for their time. Give your staff a script to help them with this. For example, you might ask them to say something like, "Hello, Mary. This is John from ABC Contracting. Is this a good time to call you?"

A script like this gives the customer the option to tell you if it is a bad time to call. The customer will respect your consideration of their time and you avoid being considered an irritant. If they say it's a good time to call, then your customer has made a positive signal for a conversation. It's like receiving an invitation rather than barging in on a party. Asking for their time makes it easy for them to receive your next call.

## Close Out Projects
The last ten percent of the job is often what is remembered most by your customer—just when everyone is out of time, money, and patience. It's a critical time of urgency and expectation for the mountain of documents required for warranties, lien waivers, certifications, as built drawings, operations and maintenance manuals plus more.

It's also the time for the final punch list, which in many cases is a subjective evaluation of your performance. I believe that the length of your punch lists are often not so much about the quality of work but rather the reward or punishment for your personal behavior during the construction phase. This is more pronounced on the architectural appearances rather than the engineered functions. It is easy to measure and accept the engineered functions of lighting brightness, power voltage, and the output of heating and air conditioning which are accepted on a pass/fail basis. Architectural measurements and acceptability, on the other hand, often lie in the mind of the beholder. Then and there the reward or punishment for your personal behavior is taken into consideration.

Those contractors deserving rewards for their good behavior will hear the owner's representative say things like: "Given the conditions you had to work in, it looks pretty good," or "For all you have done for us, we can over look that minor problem," or "We can certainly live with that."

For those contractors being punished, the owner's representative is likely to have many nitpicky comments during the punch list tour: "I don't think that wall is as straight as we expected," or "The color of the paint does not seem consistent," or "The joints in the carpet appear too obvious," or "The ceiling grid is not square enough."

Another important and well remembered part of project closeout is final payments, which sometimes include difficulty in obtaining lien waivers and the unfortunate submittal of surprise claims for extra money due to changed conditions or project delay. These events often cause destruction in the relationship and can be motivating for customers to remove contractors from future bid invitations.

To conclude this chapter I believe that employee excellence comes down to passion. Passionate employees get up extra early in the morning and can't wait to get to work. Despite all the inherent defeats and constant rigors, they go to work because they want to, not because they feel they have to. Archimedes, the great Greek mathematician and engineer in 400 B.C. said, "Give me a lever long enough and a fulcrum on which to place it, and I shall move the world." That lever and fulcrum are the passions that allow some people to achieve greatness. Passion is the fuel for the energy it takes to deal with the endless march of changes in building design, customer mood swings, site conditions and weather. Employees must know that change is a condition of life and even more so in construction. At the same time, the waves of change exist in an ocean of opportunity. Supporting employees with passion is important, because it can ignite fast as well as extinguish fast.

"The quality I look for in hiring people is a passion to win and a sense of urgency about getting it done."

> - Tim Conroy
> President, Olympic Wall Systems

"The number one reason for success as a contractor is having a good solid partnership. Integrity and honesty are imperative to communicate changes and surprises in a straightforward manner."

> - Jerry Pedlar
> Director of Facilities, North Memorial Health Care

"A person is successful if he or she possesses the inner drive to be excellent in all aspects of life and the patience to develop lasting relationships with similar-minded people. A sure cause of failure is the inability of a person to evaluate a situation from the other person's viewpoint."

> - Frank Latz
> President, Control Point Design

"There are many 'fickle' relationships out there today . . . Ten years to build something worthwhile, ten seconds to tear it down. What creates success? It's an unconditional trust between the service provider and client, where the focus and energy is centered on serving the client. We like to look at our mission statement on a regular basis to gauge our effectiveness and ultimately the success or failure of a client relationship."

> - Brian Buchholz, Principal
> BWBR Architects

# Chapter Six

# Relationship Failure

T his chapter is the ugly part of the book, and it does get ugly because it deals with the unfortunate eternal construction industry dilemma of how personal relationships with your customers are destroyed and most likely not rebuilt. This chapter is written not to denigrate or defame our industry but instead to present a situation in life that should be addressed and avoided if at all possible.

## Betrayal

So how can you alienate customers and blow up the relationship bridge? What is it that destroys so quickly what took so long to build and maintain? The destruction process can take many forms, but most all of them involve one bottom line: betrayal of trust. Betrayal is an unfortunate human experience which I believe has a particularly heavy impact upon those in the construction industry as compared to other industries. It is because of our industry's extreme reliance upon trust and the belief that contractors honor their commitments and want to be loyal.

Betrayal is more than just making a mistake or not using proper judgment on a particular issue. It results in loss of trust caused by the betrayal of the agreement that you won't take advantage of your customer's (or victim's) vulnerability. It occurs when the wrong thing is said or done to the wrong person at the wrong time and for the wrong reasons. It occurs when someone takes action to contradict a prior agreement that included a presumed level of trust.

The betrayer (perpetrator) acts as a double-crosser and takes action to favor their interest over the interest of others. They are willing to rip the skin off their customer in the futile effort to save their own. They care little about the victim because they consider their needs to be more important. To the one being betrayed it appears to be a deliberate, willful, and vindictive act. It means an immediate collapse of the previous good impressions and it dismantles optimistic expectations while leaving the victim feeling duped in the process.

Betrayal causes mental, physical and social distress. Worst yet, the applicability for the construction industry is that the more trust there is, the greater the impact of the betrayal, and thus the more distress.

I was betrayed three separate times: once by a customer, once by a business partner, and once by a subcontractor. The combined dollar amount was in excess of $10 million. The details were different but the outcomes were the same. Each instance of betrayal was a surprise, followed by the surreal reaction of "is this really happening?" I wondered why this happened and questioned if I would be able to trust again.

The mental distress from betrayal comes from anxiety: the victim's ship just sank and wrecked their mental model of expecting respect, honesty, policy, responsibility, principles and values. Betrayal victims then beat themselves up with questions and comments. "Was I naïve when I gave away my trust? How could I be so stupid as to trust him? I must have been a fool thinking I could believe him."

The physical distress for the victim is draining and comes from the feeling they were stabbed in the back. They also experience a painful churning in their stomach from the feeling of repulsion. They have a broken heart from the breach of the relationship and the treachery of being double-crossed. The social distress for the victim comes from the loss of loyalty, friendship and confidence. The victim may go into isolation to figure things out and the betrayer loses his relationships and reputation.

Those who betray have various degrees of motivation to do so.

One may do it out of panic in order to save his job: he'll sink the customer in order to stay afloat on the project budget. Others do it for more severe reasons: I know a narcissist who considers a betrayal an accomplishment and takes satisfaction from causing fear, anxiety and loss of control in others.

Once the betrayal occurs, I believe the only thing left to do for the contractor is to pack their bags and await the customer's deliverance of justice. It is their way of making right what has been wronged: not only the physical construction, but also their sensibilities.

In the construction industry, betrayal results in a permanent loss of the relationship for two reasons: first, construction requires that the contractor be trustworthy to offset the high degree of vulnerability of the customer. Second, the only thing that can mend the fence of a betrayal is love, but love exists in few construction industry relationships. There are degrees of likeability, but not love. After some resolution between the betrayer and the victim, they might shake hands with each other but it will most likely be the final handshake. They may pretend to agree to "burying the hatchet" but no shovel will be available. Why? Because the customer's negative emotions remain active and the trust is gone.

In 2000, The Society for Marketing Professional Services (SMPS), a construction-related organization, conducted a survey called "Getting from the Short List to the Contract." They asked construction clients as to why they select or reject those companies who provide professional construction services. Their reasons for rejection were not so much about capability or price but rather for arrogance, evasiveness, vagueness and bad chemistry.

## Blowing Up Bridges

Let's go back to the story in the previous chapter about the customer's conversations with his boss after awarding the contract. The bridge gets blown up when the customer's project manager gets a phone call like this one from the general contractor:

General contractor: "We have a few serious problems we need to talk about."

Customer: "Like what?"

General contractor: "We missed the third floor mezzanine on our estimate and need to raise our price."

Customer: "How could you do that? We talked about that in detail. It was supposed to be included in your price."

General contractor: "I know, but you failed to put it in writing."

Customer: "What other problems do you have to tell me about?"

General contractor: "Our foreman picked the wrong survey monuments and much of the work we installed is off the mark."

Customer: "Meaning what?"

General contractor: "We have to dismantle and reinstall much of the structural steel a few feet over and also some of the work of our subcontractors."

Customer: "I'm feeling very uncomfortable."

General contractor: "Because of that problem, we won't be able to meet the schedule we promised you."

Customer: "This better be the end of your list of problems."

General contractor: "No, there are more. In our budget estimate we mistakenly undersized the load requirements for some of the building equipment and will need a change order to upsize."

Customer: "Are you kidding?"

General contractor: "No, I'm not kidding. Plus the other factory forgot to place the order for other equipment and they won't go on overtime until you promise to pay for it."

Customer: "Why me? It's not our fault."

General contractor: "That's just the way it is."

Customer: "This call is a nightmare! What else?"

General contractor: "You told our equipment supplier not to fabricate to the drawing dimensions but they did anyway. Your prediction was right: it doesn't fit."

Customer: "I can't believe you didn't obey my orders!"

General contractor: "There are more problems."

Customer: "I can't believe you are doing this to me. I'll probably get fired over this!"

General contractor: "I hope not—but you know that change order you wouldn't approve?"

Customer: "Yes, and for good reason."

General contractor: "Well, I went over your head and called your boss. He is really upset."

Customer: "I feel betrayed!"

General contractor: "I'm sorry you feel that way, but I also have to say we forgot to pay our subcontractor and he filed a lien against the project and sent it to your boss and the bank."

Customer: "That means we can't close out the financing and lease the building. I am extremely angry right now!"

General contractor: "Well, you're probably going to get angrier. I know you want the punch list complete right away, but it will have to wait because we transferred our superintendent to another project."

Customer: "This is unbelievable. You're going to ruin me."

General contractor: "One more thing. I'm going on vacation for a few weeks and I'll try to call now and then if I get a chance. Meanwhile, can you update our new superintendent on the outstanding punch list?"

Customer: "I feel like a fool and regret trusting you."

General contractor: "Just one more thing. I know you closed out
the final budget on this job last month with our final billing
and signed lien wavers, but I forgot about the large change
order we are preparing for project delay and labor inefficiency."
Customer: "You're done with me and my company forever!"

This is obviously an extreme example where the contractor betrayed
the customer's trust on every level—however, it's clear that this
relationship was just destroyed. When trust is betrayed in these ways,
the relationship is broken forever because the customer's emotions
started on fire when his vulnerabilities were taken advantage of while
he was standing there naked, in fear of losing his job. The positive
emotions inherent in the original trust disappear and are replaced by
distress and desire for justice. Your customer's delivery of justice will
be his way to right the wrong through the satisfaction of making you
suffer in much the same degree that you made him suffer. It's a form of
revenge that is either slow and subtle or fast and direct.

Slow and subtle justice is, for example, when your company name
is removed from your customers' future bid list without informing you.
Then, when you hear about their next project and phone them for an
invitation to bid, they respond, "Whoops, we forgot to invite you, but
the number of invited bidders is full and it's too late to add any more."

The fast and direct way is when, for example, your customer calls you the next morning after staying awake most of the night, and says something like, "Hello Greg, I'm calling to direct you to remove your company's labor and equipment from the job site by the end of the day. The remainder of your work will be completed by your competitor on a time and material basis which will be paid for by your performance bond. If you want any more money out of us, including your current progress payment and retention, then you can try to sue us." The customer then puts the phone down and proceeds to send you a letter for breach of contract and is willing to badmouth your company to anyone who will listen.

## Betrayal Reactions

Remember the positive emotions linked to positive relationships described in Chapter Two? Those just got thrown out the window and replaced with negative emotions. The positive emotion of comfort in you and your company is replaced by the customer's emotion of disgust for what you did.

Expectancy that you would fulfill all that is required is replaced by hurt for believing you would protect them.

Optimism that they would look good at the end of the project is replaced by anger over the perceived deliberate harm.

Desire to get the job done as easily as possible is replaced by regret in awarding the contract to you.

Pleasure in the peace of mind that things were going well is replaced by the pain of the embarrassment you caused them.

Amazement for your going the extra mile is replaced by frustration that you created extra work for them.

Pride that they chose you for the project is replaced by alienation, resulting in closed communication.

Happiness about your personal relationship is replaced by bitterness for the betrayal of trust.

Relief that a job was going well is replaced by contempt and a desire to get even.

Passion to give you the next project is replaced by rejection from their future bid list.

Was the pursuit of the short-term gain of the betrayal worth all that?

## False Accusations

I believe the number one cause of contempt and rejection from a customer is when they are falsely accused of wrongdoing. This is received as a direct attack on their character and credibility, and the accuser will pay a heavy price.

A senior manager of a construction company was spearheading the bid preparation and hopeful negotiation for a big contract with one of their largest customers. He was very confident and verbal in telling the employees about the excellent likelihood for project award. He endorsed his confidence by pointing out his personal and business relationship with the owner of this customer's business combined with his direct intervention throughout the entire bid process. His high level of involvement was unusual, but he thought this was the win he needed to boost his image in the company.

Unfortunately, that customer called him after the bid was submitted and told the senior manager he would not receive the contract. Embarrassed and desperate to save face to his employees, the senior manager panicked and fabricated a reason why he didn't get the contract. He told employees the reason he didn't get the contract was because the customer bid shopped by leaking his bid number to the competitor, allowing them to submit a lower bid. To make matters worse, the senior manager phoned the customer and lashed out, falsely accusing him of cheating and peddling the contract to his competitor.

The customer did not respond and simply hung up the phone. He then called his senior managers to a meeting where he instructed them if they wanted to keep their jobs they could never give another contract to that company.

Ten long years later the senior manager's salesperson went back to that customer with hat in hand and asked if the relationship could be restored. The past customer said, "Sure that will be a good idea."

"That's fantastic. When can we bid your next job?"

"When your senior manager dies!"

## Failure Tips

Here are some other easy tips on how to destroy relationships with your customers:

- Whine
- Use foul language
- Discriminate against others
- Cheat on quality and safety
- Ignore their communications

- Overpromise and under-deliver
- Intimidate through force
- Execute rude collection practices
- Go over their head and play politics
- Surprise them with property liens
- Provide inconsistent communication
- Be afraid to give them important bad news
- When at the job site always blame the office
- When at the office always blame the job site
- Take advantage of their inexperienced people
- Change supervision at the last ten percent of the job
- Finger point and blame others for your actions
- Gouge them on large emergency change orders
- Barrage them with nickel-and-dime change orders
- Charge them with the duty to solve your problems
- Embarrass them in front of their peers or supervisors
- Gather half the facts and go to meetings with guns blazing
- Be too busy selling to hear what the customer wants to buy
- Practice conditional love: call only when their business is hot
- Practice ineptitude by not knowing enough about what you are trying to sell
- Be a hypocrite: brag about your company values, then do the opposite
- Take them for granted and assume you will get the next job just because

**Customer Comments**
I surveyed many owners who hired then fired general contractors because the relationship was destroyed. Below are their reasons, tied to the negative emotions of betrayal:

## Disgust
"He is smart but also very selfish and shrewd. He's a no-good phony who hides behind the cloak of acting religious."

## Hurt
"They promised me the punch list was done when in fact it wasn't and caused us great disappointment and embarrassment."

## Anger
"They thought they were the only bidder and doubled their price. Worse yet, they lied when we caught them red-handed."

## Regret
"We warned them about their project manager but they didn't listen. Dealing with this company taught me one big thing, how to suffer."

## Pain
"When I think of betrayal, I think of them."

## Frustration
"Their service was getting less and less: it was like they didn't care. Their competitor seemed more interested in our business than they did."

## Alienation
"There is something about him that I just can't trust."

## Bitterness
"They stole two of our key employees without the courtesy of talking with us first."

## Contempt
"He laid into me about not getting the last bid. He questioned my motives and defamed my character."

## Rejection
"They didn't do what I told them and it caused me great embarrassment. I told my people to kick them off the job site and never invite them back again."

## Lack of Tact

Relationships are certainly destroyed by the big hemorrhages described in this chapter, but they can also be destroyed by several tactless cuts that eventually bleed out the rapport. Tact is the ability to say and do things in a way that will not offend. It's the good use of diplomacy and consideration for the customer's position. Lack of tact is often demonstrated by multitaskers who seem to attempt to perform multiple tasks simultaneously to impress the other person with their talents in dealing with complexity.

For example, it is tactless to talk to someone while at the same time talking on your phone, going over reading material, scrolling your electronic device, or flipping through files. Instead of impressing someone, multitasking can come across as a violation of basic relational skills. It places the other person in third or fourth place for your attention when they should be first.

In addition to being rude, multitasking can also make us appear inept because our brains are not designed to effectively handle multiple mental tasks at the same time. When we attempt to multitask, the available brainpower for each task is reduced. Serious multitaskers can experience reduced concentration and memory due to the adrenaline rushes from the mental stress required to multitask. You might be taking your multitasking a bit too far if you walk into a room and can't remember what for.

I don't want to end this chapter on the sour subject of failure. However, it is important to note that employees do not need a title to make a difference by either creating success or causing failure for themselves and the company. The construction industry does not allow for many second chances because one big mistake can wipe out hundreds of congratulatory remarks. Meanwhile your competition waits around the mousetrap waiting for you to make a fatal move.

So why is being trustworthy and tactful so good and betrayal and rudeness so bad? Because if you are trustworthy and tactful, your customers will come back to you again and again, opening the doors to their hearts and projects. If you do them wrong, however, they will slam those doors shut.

"Tact is the knack of making a point without making an enemy."

- Isaac Newton 1642 - 1727

"The early bird gets the worm, but the second mouse gets the cheese."

- Jon Hammond

"Failure is caused by a breakdown of trust from not listening, poor communication, and indifference to a client's needs, leading to unclear focus and wasted energy on issues unrelated to client service."

- Brian Buchholz
Principal, BWBR Architects

Chapter Seven

# Presentations

P resentations, as described in this chapter, are the face-to-face interviews your company and your competitors have with a project owner that are usually the last step in determining who wins the prize to get the contract award. Presentations typically include a selection committee formed by the customer: the committee can include their architect, engineer, facility users, or anyone else who is a stakeholder in the project. Presenters from the general contractor typically include a senior manager, project manager, estimator and superintendent, along with anyone else who can speak to any special requirements such as safety, quality and design. It's a process that is filled with anticipation, frayed nerves and confidence (or lack thereof). The presentation results in either the thrill of victory or the agony of defeat. It's like a closing argument for an attorney where the efforts of hundreds of hours and thousands of dollars come down to the ability to persuade an audience in a short period of time.

Imagine this scenario: You become aware of an important project being negotiated and awarded before the drawings, specifications, and scope of work have yet to be totally defined. Instead of being a lump sum bid, this would be more of a partnership to determine the best scope of work for the customer's money and where your costs are reimbursed plus an additional fee amount is negotiated for reimbursement of your overhead and profit.

It's a high-trust relationship because the contract will be awarded before the total scope and dollar amounts are finalized. It's what we refer to as design build, cost plus, or negotiated fee. In order to be invited onto the bidders list, you worked hard and long to prepare a statement of qualification. As a result, you're asked to respond to a request for proposal. Success with that exercise results in your being invited to make a face-to-face presentation with the owners and others on the selection committee, who will decide who gets the project. So far, so good.

Unfortunately, you are not alone. Two of your competitors have gone through the same exercises and have also been invited to make a presentation. All three of you were invited because you are the "A-teams." Going into the presentations you are evenly matched with your competitors in the areas of budget, fees, knowledge of the scope of work, successful past projects with the owner, respectful relations with other project participants, good safety record, adequate bonding, experienced supervision, ample labor availability and high quality of work. All three of you go into the presentation room but only one comes out the winner.

How do you get to first place? This chapter will help you understand what to do and what to avoid before, during and after your presentation. You will learn the reasons why contractors do or do not get the contract award. It's not about price—instead, success or failure lies in your ability to verbally persuade, use good body language, demonstrate the credibility of your perceived competence and your willingness to have a successful project. In this chapter we'll cover:

- Why do contractors lose the award?
- Why do contractors get the award?
- Effective persuasion
    ethos
    pathos
    logos
- Before the presentation
- During the presentation
- After the presentation
- If you fail

## Why Do Contractors Lose the Award?

I interviewed selection committee members to ask why they did not select certain contractors. Here are some of their comments:

- Their president was so arrogant you could feel it when he walked into the room.
- The wrong person hogged the whole presentation.
- They felt too sure about getting the job, but did not demonstrate enough effort.
- I didn't feel like I could get along with the foreman.
- They gave too many evasive answers.
- They did not accurately respond to our request for proposal.
- Lack of tact and poor people skills.
- We told them we didn't like their project manager and they still put him on the proposed team.
- They didn't listen to us.
- They didn't act like they were that interested—the project manager was bored.
- They didn't understand the project.
- We were suspicious that we'd see a lot of nickel-and-dime change orders.
- They were busy and out of "A team" players, and it looked like they came with the "C team."
- They've been doing our work for years, almost exclusively. They acted like they were entitled to this next big project and didn't put forth the effort. Their competition did a much better presentation.
- They went above my head and around my back.
- They were rude to our receptionist, and only nice to us.
- They assumed the relationship was stronger than it was, and felt we should pay a premium for a relationship that didn't exist.

- We gave them time to set up the room the way they wanted, and they couldn't even coordinate that among themselves.
- They gave us a presentation to build our church and one guy tried to act as if he was more Catholic than the Pope.
- It wasn't any big thing in particular, just a general sense that they were going through the motions and didn't offer us anything new.

Not only did these contractors not get the contracts awarded to them, their behavior left a lasting bad impression. They left those potential customers feeling that their time was wasted and their wants and needs were ignored.

**Why Do Contractors Get the Award?**

It's often difficult to learn exactly why a contractor was awarded a particular contract, because the reasons are often private, stemming from the heart and not the head. The positive reasons are also difficult to uncover because the customers are concerned that the reason may come across as favoritism. It is uncomfortable for them to admit that they don't know exactly why they made a decision. Still, it's very common for selection committee members to say something like, "I don't really know why, but I felt more comfortable with ABC contractor than XYZ."

I've also heard this kind of a reason from selection committee members: "Among the three presenters, two of them blew their presentation. We awarded to the one who made the fewest mistakes." Such an award by default does not provide an opportunity to make a proud announcement.

Here are some other reasons selection committee members have given for making an award:

- They were honest in answering the tough questions about the schedule even though they knew we would not like the answer.
- I felt we could trust them most to look out for us. They know how to listen and they gave us great advice. Very professional and knowledgeable.

- They dug into the job more than the others. They acted like they really wanted it, and it showed. Their whole team was in the same boat.

- We invited extra new bidders and found out how fortunate we are with our regular contractor. We realize now that we should not try to fix something that isn't broken.

## Effective Persuasion

The Greek philosopher Aristotle divided the ways to persuade people into three categories: ethos, pathos and logos. Ethos refers to ethics. Ethos is the means by which you establish credibility and your competence to do the job at hand. Pathos refers to passion or emotion. In this context, pathos is how you establish your willingness to do the best job possible. Logos refers to logic, which is the means by which you demonstrate your ability to do the job. Pathos is about your willingness to have a successful project whereas logos is about your ability to have a successful project. Ethos is about the integrity that allows you the opportunity to persuade them about your willingness and ability.

In order to succeed, your presentations must use all three principles to persuade the customer that you are the right choice for their project.

Most presentations fail because the presenter skips the first two types of persuasion and jumps right into trying to convince the buyer logically. It's true that many customers decide from the left side of their brain (logic, facts, and numbers) and award the project based on logos: a logical justification that you are able to meet the budget, scope and quality of the plans and specifications. Many customers, however, decide with the right side of their brain (feelings, imagination and big picture). To convince these buyers, you must speak from passion, using the principle of pathos to help them believe that you will look out for their best interest and not take advantage of them.

Both sides of their brains need the ethos section of the presentation, which assures them that you are competent and honest. Pathos people are typically the managers who seek the vision and imagination of a successful project. Logos people are typically the architects and engineers whose duty it is to assure adherence to plans and specifications.

## Ethos

Ethos is your credibility, reputation and ethical appeal. You first need to convince your audience that you are worth listening to, likable and worthy of respect. First impressions are lasting impressions. You must establish that you are honest, forthright and a reliable source for the information in your presentation. This can't be faked because people can instantly spot insincerity, arrogance and deceitfulness.

Credibility is established by demonstrating intelligence, virtue and goodwill. This can be established through confident verbal tone and positive body language while you present your technical expertise and vested interest in the project. Presenting your previous record of integrity is required to convince them you will do them no harm. One company representative demonstrated ethos when he told the selection committee, "I have thirty years of experience. I had direct supervision over this estimate and will also have daily guardianship over the project manager for this project."

When he was asked what his position was with the company he replied: "I own it."

## Pathos

Pathos is your ability to appeal to the emotions and imagination of your audience. What is in their best interest and most advantageous for them? What are the shared values and why are they important? Use vivid description and emotional language.

During the presentation for a major hospital renovation, the customer asked one contractor's superintendent why they should choose his company for the project. He responded: "I was born in this hospital thirty-five years ago. I owe something back to you. I will take care of this project with the same care and respect that you gave me on the day I was born."

The contractor was successful in winning the contract because the presentation tapped into the emotions of trust and respect. This is a great example of using the principle of pathos.

**Logos**
Logos is persuading by the use of reasoning. It's using logic to back up your claims with supporting evidence: hard facts, material quantities, labor hours and other numbers plus letters of recommendation from your peers. Successful presenters are able to say: "We have been in business for so many years and have successfully completed many projects just like this one. We have completed all of them ahead of schedule, below budget and without any lost time injuries. We never had a change order dispute or a project lien. Here are the phone numbers of five of your peers who would surely recommend us for your project."

**Ethos:** Ethics > Credibility > Reputation
**Pathos:** Passion > Emotion > Willingness
**Logos:** Logic > Facts > Ability

# Body Language

Body language is one of the most important components of persuasion. It is what enables you to use the three principles of ethos, pathos, and logos to convince the customer that you are the best choice for the project. Body language includes your facial expressions, physical movements and tone of voice. Although much of body language is subconscious, paying attention to your own emotions and state of mind during the presentation will ensure that your body language backs up what you have to say.

Body language is woven into our genes and even today represents about sixty percent of our communication. About thirty percent of the

meaning is conveyed by the pitch, tone, and volume of your voice—
which leaves only about ten percent for the actual spoken words.

What is body language? Body language is any body movement or
facial expression which sends a message. It is an essential element in
social and business interactions. It is a subconscious and spontaneous
action expressing some emotion. Body language can express the
difference between verbal statements and thoughts and feelings.
The ability to read and translate body language is important in the
construction industry because so often what is really being said is not
coming from the mouth but rather from the movement of the body.
How to use body language in your presentation will be addressed later
on in the chapter.

## Before the Presentation

In preparation, make sure you include ethos, pathos and logos. This
presentation is the home stretch. It may only allow you thirty to sixty
minutes to persuade the audience in your favor. It's the culmination
of all the efforts of senior managers who wrote the proposals and
qualification statements that got you this far, and the time spent by the
estimators in budgeting and value engineering, the time spent by the
project manager in determining scope of work and requirements for
safety, quality, and schedule, plus the time spent by the superintendent
in visiting the job site and becoming familiar with the conditions and
logistics.

If the presentation focuses on the introduction of your team
(pathos), then prepare for a conversation about shared values, customer
loyalty, problem solving and your trustworthiness. I don't suggest
preparing a PowerPoint presentation for this section, because the
technology on the screen will distract your audience from the human
side of your presentation.

Instead, prepare to invite a casual two-way conversation. This
should be more of a "get-to-know-you" presentation than the "we-talk-
and-you-listen" variety. This is prompted by you asking them questions
about what is in their best interest and how they will measure success

at the end of the project. Talking about the end of the project may send a subconscious message to the customer that you already have the job. They may tell themselves: "As long as they have already built this in their head we might as well give them the contract."

If the presentation is going to focus on scope of work and numbers (logos) then prepare detailed documents, specifications, and spreadsheets, and bring a calculator. I do suggest PowerPoint presentations in this case, but make it simple and easy to read. Display it for only as long as required so the audience can get back to focusing on you and not being bored with the screen.

Act like you want the job, even before the presentation. Some decision makers think you are only going through the process because of the owner's requirement to get three proposals. Visit the site and meet the people you will be working with. Look for questions to ask the customer afterward on a one-on-one basis. That way the customer will realize you were thinking and interested rather than just walking around.

Don't assume you know the customer's wants and needs and categorize them for both the short- and long-term. "Wants" are usually the things they can't afford and "needs" are the things they have to have. Protect the budget by giving what they need first and then see if they can afford their wants.

Realize that through the prequalification stage they already know what you can do. Prepare to tell them how you are going to do it. Assume that safety, quality, and schedule are their minimal expectations. If this is your first invitation, determine if they are having a problem with your on-site competitor. Owners are usually willing to let teams stay together as long as they are able to work together.

Research your competitor's weaknesses, and highlight your unique capabilities. Know your competitor's strengths and try to either match or neutralize them. If your competitor's weakness is from a betrayal, then emphasize your values.

Ask for an agenda. If they don't have one, ask if you can prepare one. Ask what they want you to bring such as drawings, charts, schedules, or handouts.

Determine who should attend by asking who will attend from the customer's side and mirroring them. For example, if they have attendees who are concerned with schedule, safety and field supervision then bring your people with parallel responsibilities.

Rehearse ahead of time and have an observer play the role of the customer by asking questions and giving both positive and negative feedback.

If possible, prepare bullet line notes instead of text and don't read from them. If possible, visit the room you will be presenting in to determine the logistics for viewing, electrical outlets, screen size and thermostat.

Focus your preparation on ways to promote a conversation, not on documents. Determine the questions to ask in order to get dialogue going. Be careful about too much glitz. Customers like to buy but don't like to be sold.

Remember that they don't expect your superintendent or project manager to be professional speakers. Instead, they want to get a feel for your project manager and superintendent, whom they may not have met. In addition to their experience they will look for trust, openness, confidence and loyalty.

Separate your team from the commodity of your business. Your brick, mortar, steel, lights, plumbing, windows, and so on are all specified and will be perceived and expected as being no different than your competitor.

Prepare for the tough questions and decide who will answer each one. Here are some of the questions I've faced at presentations in the past. I suggest that you think through an answer for each of them and decide who is the best person to deliver that information.

- Why is your price the highest?
- Tell me about your company in one minute or less.
- What are your company values?
- What is your policy on ethics and accountability?
- What do you see as the biggest challenge?
- How will you handle street and foot traffic?

- What is your approach to value engineering?
- What is your experience in working with a new customer?
- What is your experience in working with the architect and engineer?
- What is the benefit to using self-performed labor? What is the detriment?
- How would you work with an owner's representative?
- Explain how you recovered from a major mistake.
- What would your customer say about your last project?
- What do you know about the regulatory agencies involved?
- What is your definition of collaboration?
- Describe your community involvement?
- Explain your crisis management plan?
- What distinguishes you from your competitors?
- When was the last time you were in litigation and why?
- Are you willing to go open book?
- How are you going to handle change orders?
- Give one big reason why we should pick you?

Don't play politics by going around the back or over the head of those on the award committee. Doing so shows lack of respect for those on the committee and also sends a message that your company is weak and needs the help of others to prop you up.

Don't prepare for your marketing director to dominate the show. This is about where the rubber meets the road with your project manager and field supervision.

Acknowledge Murphy's Law and plan for something to go wrong. Be prepared to handle it in a calm way, with humor if possible. How you react to a mishap at the presentation will demonstrate to the selection committee how you will react to problems during the project. Don't miss this invaluable opportunity to perform.

Bring an extra light bulb for your projector. Assume you will lose your internet connection, someone will forget their notes or a key document, and someone else will get lost or delayed in traffic. A calm and controlling statement could be: "Well, this goes to show how change is inherent in construction and we'll simply adapt to it."

---

**Always proofread carefully to see if you any words out.**

---

Preparing to answer questions can also avoid self-destruct answers. Let's say you get this question: "How are you going to handle change orders?" The wrong answer is to have your team members all stare at each other with worried eyes, begging for someone else to hold the bomb. Then one of your brave team members says: "Uh, we will handle them one at a time."

Oops. That answer just signaled to the selection committee that you are prepared to nickel-and-dime your way out of the project by demanding a change order for anything and everything that changes.

What is the right answer? "Although we are very able and adaptable, it is our preference to avoid change orders because they disrupt the sequence of work, delay the schedule, and cost both of us extra money. Plus they provide an opportunity for a disagreement that we don't want to happen. However, we all realize that, yes, there probably will be changes. When that happens we will work to making the changes more responsive to the eventual project needs."

A possible answer to the question, "Give one big reason why we should pick you," might not be to recite your company mission statement. Instead try something more personal, like: "The function of my company is to feed, clothe and house my family. The way I personally accomplish this is by providing maximum gain to the people who choose to work with me."

Finally, be well informed and cautious in your decision whether or not to offer gifts at the end of your presentation to members of the selection committee. Giving gifts, such as your promotional items, can result in two negative consequences. The first is the perception by committee members that you are trying to manipulate or sway their decision in your favor through the proposition of a gift—instead of being appreciative they are often instead insulted. The other negative response could be an automatic disqualification of your company for offering gifts in a type or dollar amount that exceeds their company policy. This violation of policy can also remove you company name from future bid invitations. So be careful: spending money on gifts could be the worst money you ever spend.

## During the Presentation

Here is where the rubber meets the road and where you need to hit a home run. Your audience will be observing your logos, pathos and ethos by listening not only to what you say but also how you say it— tone of voice and body language are critical here. Is your ethos coming across as being credible or suspicious? Is your pathos appealing to their positive or negative emotions? Is your logos persuading them with firm facts or vague answers?

Realize that you have a short amount of time to present what it will be like to work with your company for a long time. You have only one chance to make a good first impression and that usually happens within the first ten seconds. When meeting someone for the first time, I am usually able to quickly perceive their degree of friendliness, trustworthiness, assertiveness and capability. If you don't make a good first impression, you probably won't have a second chance to change it. It takes five positive encounters to cancel one negative encounter.

Basic courtesy can take you a long way. Above all, follow these suggestions to get the meeting off to a good start. These are invaluable opportunities to display respect to the customer.

- Be polite to the receptionist. Assume they will ask her how she was treated.
- Turn off all electronic devices. If you forget and it rings, do not answer it.
- Insert all of your presenter's calling cards in one clear plastic window packet.

- Accept offers of water or coffee with yes, please, and thank you. Starting a meeting with yes sets a welcoming and positive tone.
- Take the water: coffee can give you bad breath.
- Don't assume they have read your proposal or that they think you want the job.
- Act like you really want the job. Sit up straight, act confident, and wear a smile.
- Display energy: interest can quickly fade to boredom.

When presenting, know your room and know your audience. If you have technical people in the audience, show them your abilities. If there are finance people in the audience, give them your estimating and tracking reporting abilities. Don't apologize for being nervous, turn it into positive energy. Make sure that there is room for everyone in your presentation team to speak. Show coordinated teamwork. Your customer will extrapolate from the presentation to the way you will work together on the job site.

Remember that strict rules and procedures are usually not the answer. Instead, go with your natural instincts rather than sounding like a trained choir. Stay clear of using a cleverly-worded corporate mission statement. Mission statements can sound very hollow when the management is not sincere or may sound like it was created at one of those all-day company development marathons.

Present your company with contagious business techniques and show that you empower your employees to make a difference. They are the team that the owners are really looking at, not the chief officers. Separate from your competitors by offering something unique that is beyond their expectations.

## Present According to Your Roles

Each presentation is unique, therefore each requires unique attention and decisions on who is going to attend from your company. Most presentations require a minimum of a senior manager, project manager, estimator, and superintendent. The reason for such a variety is that nobody knows everything in this business. Your audience will not expect that just one person from your company will know everything and be able to answer all the questions.

Don't feel bad about bringing a full team. It will show that you have a strong bench within your company. Team members can also provide strong emotional support and build upon each other's statements throughout the presentation.

Everyone who speaks should be able to inspire trust and comfort by demonstrating respect, rapport, shared values, responsiveness, and empathy.

Here's a list of some key players and their roles in the presentation.

## Principal

Companies that want the job bring the boss along. The principal's job is to make introductions, address key players, summarize, commit to the project, and to ask for the order. The principal should observe the positive and negative body language of the customers for their summary remarks. He might use phrases like: "We wish to highlight . . . We are concerned we didn't fully cover . . . There may have been some confusion." Doing so will allow him to address areas where enthusiasm, resistance or confusion was noticed or identified.

## Marketing and Sales

In the presentation, the marketing and sales staff should have a limited role. They got you to the presentation, now is the time for marketing and sales to back off and let the others do their part.

## Estimators

The role of the estimators is to clarify the scope of work for the customer's best interest, not your company's. If there is something wrong in the specifications, or if some feature is too expensive for their budget, it's the estimator's job to tell them and offer a solution, an alternative, or a workaround.

**Project Manager and Superintendents**
Their role is to discuss what they will do and how they will do it.
They should demonstrate passion, confidence, and dependability. They
should meet potential problems with solutions, urgency, common sense
and a positive attitude.

## Use and Observe Body Language

At your presentation, use positive body language to signal confidence,
honesty and cooperation. Give them a firm handshake while looking
them in the eye. Lean forward in your seat with legs uncrossed. Use
free movement of hands and arms. Put your hand on your chest when
being very sincere.

In addition, read your customer's body language to know when you
are having the right effect. Here are some examples of body language
that indicates they are interested in what you are saying:
• hand gripping chin
• tilted head
• nodding yes
• raised eyebrows
• squinting
• eye contact
• glasses in mouth and taking notes
When you see these signs, keep going.

Here are some examples of body language that indicates disinterest
or boredom:
• shuffling papers
• cleaning fingernails
• palm under chin
• lack of eye contact
• looking at the door or window
• picking at clothes
• doodling
• drumming fingers on the table

- tapping feet
- pen clicking
- the most obvious: sleeping

When you see these signs, change the subject or move on.

Here are some examples of body language that indicate confusion, uncertainty and doubt:
- pinching the bridge of the nose with eyes closed
- fingers to mouth
- biting lip
- scratching head
- head down
- a look of concern or puzzlement
- leaning back in the chair
- crossed legs
- red face

When you see these signs, clarify what's being said.

Body language that says be quiet and listen is the steepled hands, a triangle with finger tips raised and touching while the palm is down. This language is used by people in high authority to express superiority by saying, I'm up here and you are down below me. When you see this, give that person a good listen and then acknowledge what they say, agreeing with them if possible.

## Maximize Your Speaking Skills

Keep in mind that the number one fear for the majority of people is public speaking—which means you already have something important in common with your upcoming audience.

A nervous stomach is normal and gives you energy. Even the good experienced professional speakers have nervous stomachs before their speeches. Many who say they don't are often also the ones who are stiff and boring.

The best presentation tool you can bring with you is confidence.

This is easily attained by focusing on two things: preparation and limiting your speaking role to only those points that you are familiar with. It's not a deposition, so be friendly and relaxed. The mere fact that they invited you means they want you there and are interested in what you have to say. You are there to increase your image and credibility beyond your competitors by sounding intelligent and confident with the ability to listen and answer questions in a short and direct manner.

Capitalize on those silent moments to emphasize what is important in what you have to say and as an opportunity to prompt the customer's comments and questions: they will fill up the silence with valuable information. Silence and attentive listening lead customers to the realization that you care about what they have to say.

Though the presentation is very serious business, try to induce humor when appropriate. People with a sense of humor are more readily accepted and are able to reduce the stress of the presentation.

## What Not to Do

Do not use "in phrases" that might bother them such as:
- absolutely
- at the end of the day
- by and large
- excellent
- like
- no problem
- out-of-the-box thinking
- per se
- state-of-the-art
- that being said
- the takeaway
- ya know what I mean

It isn't that the phrases are bad or improper, but for some people, they have the same effect as fingernails on a chalkboard. For others it may be that someone who bothers them uses those phrases and you may be branded with the same stigma.

Some actions will destroy your credibility and forecast your future negative dealings. In order to succeed at presentations, never respond to questions in these ways:

- bragging
- bluffing
- shooting from the hip
- evading a question
- guessing
- making promises that can't be kept

If you don't know the answer to their question, then tell them you don't know and assure them you will get back to them with an answer. Use the follow-up as an opportunity for further discussions. Or it is perfectly acceptable to defer a question to a more qualified team member.

Experienced people know that the more you know about construction, the more you realize how much there is still left to learn.

Do not ask their opinion about any documents you may have submitted prior to this presentation. They may not have read it, which will result in embarrassment to both parties.

Do not tell them you are going to take charge of the project unless you know they want you to.

Presentations are often ruined by actions like these:

**Name Dropping**
Your mention of a person who is important can be taken negatively. It may be viewed as you having a low ego and are attempting to manipulate through superiority in order to impress someone.

**Criticizing Your Competition**
Remember, they got invited too and being critical will likely offend the customer and makes him pass judgment on you.

## Talking Forever or Talking Over Other Participants
It's essential to show respect for other people in this process, whether they are your colleagues, your competitors, or your customers.

## Using Foul Language
You have a very good chance of offending someone by using anything other than businesslike, friendly language. Swearing also diminishes and cheapens what's being said and puts your credibility in question as someone who needs to use foul language in order to express yourself.

## Using the "I" Word.
Saying "I built the X project" conveys that you are not a team player and have an exaggerated ego.

Other very disrespectful actions include looking out the window while others are talking, and going over your allotted time. Again, respecting other people demands that you respect their time. Everyone is busy.

And finally, the two most important things: don't forget to thank them for their time and also ask for the contract. Do not press hard, but instead say something like: "We don't want to appear pushy but we are asking for the job and are ready to start as soon as you are ready to say go."

# Use the Emotional Buying Motivators

Remember the ten emotional buying factors presented in Chapter 2? These are the emotions you want your customers to experience over time in their relationships with your company. You want your customers to walk out of the presentation having experienced these feelings. For each job, some will be more important than others: sense what's most important to the decision-makers on the selection committee. What are their primary concerns? Whenever you're in doubt about what to present or how to respond, address those concerns and foster these feelings in your customers.

- comfort
- expectancy
- optimism
- desire
- pleasure
- amazement
- pride
- happiness
- relief
- passion

### Comfort

To help the buyer feel comfortable about working with you and your company, say something like, "We will commit our A-team to this project, with the full confidence that you will be impressed with both the engineering and architectural features."

### Expectancy

Help the customer confidently look forward to seeing your company fulfill all that's required. For example, you might say something like, "We reviewed the drawings with all the parties and user groups and do not expect any change orders. You should also not expect to see any punch list as we will perfect our work as it is installed."

### Optimism

Help the customer anticipate how they will look good at the end of the project. For example: "We have done many serious projects like this before, and not only for you, but also many similar customers. We will not affect your 24/7 operations or bog you down with negativity. We practice win-win."

### Desire

Understand the customer's craving to get the project done as easily as possible. Give your customer this kind of message: "We have spent a lot of time determining your wants and needs and wishes. We will not have to bother you to satisfy those. You can simply relax and wait for us to complete the project."

### Pleasure

Pleasure is the customer's contentment in the peace of mind that things will go well. Let the customer understand that you have checked and double-checked every procedure and specification on this project and have scheduled every activity, including subcontractor and material suppliers. You want them to get this message: "We have essentially built this job before it will ever start. You will be gratified that this project will be about both business and pleasure."

### Amazement

Amazement is the customer's high regard for you going the extra mile. Here's an example: "The drawings you provided were not complete, but we took the extra steps to complete them and can give you a guaranteed maximum price. Also, even though it's not required in your specifications, we will have our project manager on site fulltime."

### Pride

Give the customer an opportunity to be proud about awarding you the project in exchange for the self-respect and high esteem they envision receiving at the end of the project. After receiving the contract award you want your customer to say with stateliness to their peers: "We invited only the best contractors to be considered for this project and we awarded it to the best of the best."

### Happiness

Happiness is the joy stemming from the achievement of a personal relationship. It's a reciprocal connection bonded by the appreciation and gratitude resulting from helping them. You want your customer to say: "We would be happy to award you the contract because we appreciate what you have done and what you will do."

## Relief

Alleviating the customer's anxiety that the project will not be successful spells relief. The customer knows they have problems that they cannot tackle by themselves, and they want the relief of knowing they can trust you to solve them. The message you want to convey is something like this: "We already know what the problems are and we have at least two solutions for each. Because of our shared values we will not surprise you, embarrass you, or hurt your excellent reputation."

## Passion

This is the supreme emotion. It's the customer's enthusiastic willingness (pathos) to give you the contract because both parties are agreed and prepared to be mutually successful. It's the eagerness to get started on winning. Your customer will say: "Let's get started on this ASAP so we can both be profitable." Passion is also what gets you the next contract after this one.

Failure is what you leave behind after your presentation. Owners want to see a team that can coordinate and command. You are being hired to successfully manage the project for the owner. Leave them with confidence your team has that talent. Never talk of your past projects in "what we learned" lessons. That just shows you have not completed your full skillsets.

When presenting, know your room, and know your audience. If you have technical people show them your abilities, if you have finance people in the audience give them your estimating and tracking reporting abilities. Don't apologize for being nervous: turn it into positive energy. Let all in your presentation team speak. Rehearse to show a coordinated team and don't leave failure behind.

- Bill Dunham RET
Director of Design and Construction,
Allina Hospitals and Clinics

## After the Presentation

Celebrate or complain to one another in the parking lot, but don't let
the customer see it. When you get back to the office keep working
and show interest, but don't be a pest. Debrief each other in a mature
and honest way to determine the positives and negatives of both your
verbal presentation and your body language. Where did you impress,
surprise, evade, or disappoint? Follow up with a call or thank you letter
reaffirming the positive and clarifying or neutralizing the negative.

### What the Customers Will Say About You After the Presentation

Typically the selection committee will gather and ask themselves
questions to determine if you have qualified to win the award. They
may not be conscious of it, but their questions will fall into the three
categories of ethos, pathos and logos. The better you can do on these
questions, the more likely your company is to be awarded the contract.

Here are some of the questions your customers will ask themselves
that fall under the principle of ethos:

- Were they convincing and worth listening to?
- Did they demonstrate virtue and goodwill?
- Were they confident in both verbal and body language
  communication?
- Did they work as a team?
- Did they work hard or just fake it?
- Does their story fit?
- Are they willing to communicate bad news?

Under the principle of pathos, customers will ask themselves
questions like these:

- Do they share our values?
- Are they looking out for our best interest?
- Do they have a personal stake in our project?

- Will they make us look good at the end of the project?
- What does your gut tell you?

Customer questions like these can be categorized under the principle of logos:

- Do the costs seem appropriate?
- Does the schedule seem logical?
- Can they comply with our safety and quality requirements?
- Are they current in technology for design, estimating, scheduling, cost control and billing?
- Did they identify and quantify the risk and potential changes?
- Does everything make sense and is it measurable?

When rehearsing for your presentations have an observer use the ethos, pathos, logos milestone measurements above as a checklist to ensure that each of your presenters is responsible for positive answers to those questions.

## If You Are Not Selected

Don't call and whine or condemn when asking why you didn't get the job. They probably won't give the real reason if it was made on an emotional level. Those hunches or gut feelings are hard to describe and awkward to justify to the concerned second and third place finishers. Don't accuse them of wrongdoing—that will result in a rejection of all future bid invitations. They will also appreciate the enjoyment of telling others how unqualified you are.

Instead ask for an informal meeting to show respect and learn from your mistakes. Ask how you could do better, or what else they would have liked to see or hear from you. Discover if the reason for not being selected was for being in the category of either "not selected" or "rejected." Being not selected probably indicates your competitor did a better job and therefore was the best choice. Being rejected, on the other hand, is probably due to some significant fault in your presentation that disqualified you. Not being selected means you have to improve your presentation tactics whereas being rejected means you need to change your presentation tactics. That will get you in a better position for the next project presentation.

# Chapter Eight

# Boiling It Down

Here we are at the end of the book. You have read many things, both little and big, about what to do and not to do in order to succeed as a general contractor. You might ask, "What does it boil down to? What is the one thing I should concentrate on in order to create success and avoid failure?"

Obviously there is no one factor that guarantees success or ensures failure in construction. If there were, I wouldn't have needed to write this book! If forced to sum it all up, though, I would say that honesty is the best quality to take on the route to success.

Honesty, in this case, is defined as the willingness to recognize your personal strengths and weaknesses, along with the ability to maximize those strengths through leadership and minimize your weaknesses through education and delegation. Honesty means having integrity and being truthful in your dealings with employees and customers. Honesty is analogous to construction itself: "The manner in which something is built."

Building the organization and customer relations requires that you make good on promises. Honesty is the basis and prerequisite for leadership and therefore the ability to successfully manage relationships. Without honesty there is no trust or respect and therefore no ability to influence others to follow you. Honesty also means giving merit upon the receipt of good news. Prizing honesty allows others to be open when delivering bad news, even when it hurts.

> In NASA, we never punish error. We only punish the
> concealment of error.
>
> – Al Siepert

Conversely, arrogance is the trait most responsible for failure. Honesty is an all-or-nothing character trait, but arrogance is practiced in varying degrees. It is beyond self-confidence, and those with gross arrogance take pleasure in thinking the best person is the one in the mirror. In meetings with employees and customers, they act as if they are the most important and smartest person in the room. They do not let their lack of knowledge prevent them from being an expert and have no hesitation suppressing others by embellishing their flawed opinions.

When managers are arrogant, employees will not follow them off the proverbial cliff. They have difficulty playing the required subservient role to the customer. Also, arrogant people often view a differing opinion as a personal attack. They disdain other perspectives and treat interpersonal relationships with an adversarial perspective. They dismantle teamwork, which makes them the opposite of being constructive.

Leadership theorists suggest we are all servants to someone, or we should be. When working with a win-win attitude, in serving others, we serve the good of the whole.

Most people don't want to be associated with arrogance. Arrogant management fails in construction and in life most often because you can't be a leader if no one is following. Arrogance can be easily spotted. I recall a construction manager who described his impression of a contractor he just met by saying: "I could tell that project manager was arrogant from the first time I met him, just by the swagger in his walk."

A contractor's company must choose to either obey or disobey the obligation to practice proper conduct towards fellow employees and customers. I believe the practice or non-practice of the social ethic within the company determines success or failure.

As you begin to process this knowledge and experience, I want to leave you with six tips that apply not just to construction, but to life as well. I hope they will help you succeed at construction, but even more than that, I hope they will help you look back with few regrets once you retire.

- Adjust your attitude
- Take time
- Leave the job at work
- Perseverance and purpose
- Do good
- Share your gifts with people

## Adjust Your Attitude

Success is propelled by positive self-fulfilling prophecy. It is the self-proclaimed prediction that alters your actions and causes itself to come true. A self-fulfilling prophecy is a conscious message sent to the subconscious part of your brain. Self-fulfilling prophecy will produce either a good or bad outcome depending on the forecast. Whether you decide to focus on the good or the bad, your focus will consume your character and determine your destiny. The fact that we have the ability to think also means we have the ability to control our thoughts. Therefore, your attitude is either the lock or the key to your success. Your dreams, success and fortune are not certain but are the result of attitude, so consciously send messages of success to your brain. Allow yourself to be optimistic and to expect good things.

At work, if you think you will not get the next bid, then you are right. Positive or negative self-talk becomes reinforced into the paradigm that you have determined and then produces evidence to support your belief. To support your belief that you will not be awarded the next bid award, you will sabotage yourself by proclaiming your competition has a better chance, your relationship is not strong enough, you are just going through a budgeting exercise and low price is the only factor. You will ignore any buying signal that will place you in a competitive advantage because you must prove you are right about not getting the job.

Instead practice the discipline of positive self-fulfilling prophecy that will increase your chance for success. This is so important, because winners tend to continue winning.

For example, here are some ways to reverse non-productive negative thoughts. When you find yourself with the first thought in your mind, substitute the second one.

- Instead of *I'm not perfectly qualified* think *I'm the one who can do this.*
- Instead of *I won't get a pay raise* think *I deserve a big one.*
- Instead of *I'll probably fail* think *I'll do great.*
- Instead of *People won't agree with me* think *I'll be persuasive.*
- Instead of *I don't have a college degree* think *I'll use my street smarts and experience.*
- Instead of *We could lose big money on this job* think *We will manage the risk and surprises.*

> "Always bear in mind that your own resolution to succeed is more important than any one thing."
> - Abraham Lincoln (1809-1865)

Yes, this may sound like self-cheerleading on your conscious level, but your brain absolutely believes those positives on your subconscious level and will help you carry it out. Positive thinking is not about fooling yourself—rather it's about creating yourself. A big step in this mindset is obtaining self-confidence—the ability to trust yourself in the belief that you can attain your ambitions with eyes wide open about the challenges ahead. Aristotle philosophized that all human actions have one or more of these seven causes: chance, nature, compulsion, habit, reason, passion and desire.

Dr. Dennis Waitley, past Chairman of Psychology for the U.S. Olympic Committee, counselor to POWs from Vietnam and Apollo Astronauts, produced an audio series titled *The Psychology of Winning*. He takes the word "responsibility" and changes it to "response-ability," meaning the ability to respond to situations either optimistically or pessimistically. Dr. Waitley found that winners by and large responded to situations optimistically and said: "Being a winner is an attitude, a way of life, a self-concept. It's a heads-up, full speed ahead way of living and being."

Dr. Waitley taught me to pay great attention to the power of optimism and pessimism because we have three types of occurrences in life: The first is what happens to us. The second is what we bring into our life. The third is our response to the things that happen to us.

The word optimist comes from the Latin word *optimus* meaning best. Optimists believe people and events are inherently good and the world is a positive place where most situations work out for the best. They expect the most favorable result in everything they do. They expect good things—such as a good day, the next contract, a promotion, a good parking spot, good health, friends and humor—and they usually get them.

The word pessimist is from the Latin word *pessimus* meaning worst. Pessimists believe the world is bad and getting worse. Evil will triumph over good and they are resigned to defeat without offering positive suggestions. They expect the least favorable result in everything they do. They predict a bad day, failure, frustration, more problems, bad service and enemies—and they often get them.

Your choice of reacting optimistically or pessimistically is the ultimate freedom that nobody can take away from you regardless of your situation. Yes, there are many bad surprises that a positive attitude can't prevent but, when they happen, you'd better be positioned to have your attitude and perspective on top of a ladder rather than in a ditch. In planning your future, remember that we don't get out of life what we hope or wish for, but rather what we expect and earn. Realize that the best thing or the worst thing in your life could be your attitude.

## Take Time to Make Time

Years ago the Little River Band had a song called "Lady." The first
verse says:

*Look around you, look up here.*
*Take time to make time, make time to be there.*
*Look around, be a part.*
*Feel for the winter, but don't have a cold heart.*

These lyrics teach the importance of intentionally taking time out.
They tell you to empathize with people affected by harsh events, but
not to let them drag your heart down. So yes, take time to make time
and make that time to be there just for you—and don't feel guilty
about it.

When you take time for yourself, let yourself appreciate the exact
moment you are in. Don't think about what you are supposed to do
fifteen minutes from now, or a day or week later. Don't act like children
who get in the car on a trip and soon say, "Are we there yet?" Instead,
think about where you are right now as your destination. Yes, it's
important to be responsible and plan for your future, but you don't have
to be planning every minute. That way you can pay attention to what
you have to appreciate in this present moment, instead of focusing
on what you hope for in the future. Thinking in the moment relieves
anxiety because you are not agonizing over the past or worrying about
the future.

Realize that life should be more about things to enjoy rather than
a list of things to do. Our society has high regard for those who are
successful and dedicated to the pursuit of that success. But staying busy
on the endless treadmill for the sake of staying busy does not guarantee
that success.

Being too busy can make you act stupid and dangerous because
your mind is someplace other than where it should be. Some of my
stupid acts when too busy include asking my wife where my car keys
are and she says, "In your hand." Another time I left the gas station
with the pump hose still connected to the car. Yet another time I paid
for fast food at the pay window then driving right past the pickup
window empty-handed.

Busyness is the thief that robs you of the most important things in life such as health, family and friends. Take a well-deserved and probably long-overdue personal break every day, even if for a small amount of time. Go ahead and schedule time to recognize and appreciate balance, peace, creativity, potential, options and your freedoms.

## Leave the Job at Work

Unless you've had a super day at work I believe it is best to leave your job out of your home. Why drag a bad day into your home when it can be left outside and ready for pickup the next morning? The amount of time between leaving work and getting home is a good time to transition from *work* mode to *home* mode. Remember what is important to you—friends, family, home—and leave the job behind.

Sometimes the job wants to follow you home and get inside your house. When this happens you can play a healthy imaginary trick on yourself by taking your job and holding it with your thumb and index finger. Then, before entering your home, place your job on a plant or light fixture which allows the stress of the job to drain away from you. When you're leaving for work the next day, pick it up and take it to work with you. You might be surprised that nothing happened overnight.

If you insist on taking your job home with you after a bad day, then try not to take it to bed with you. Problems seem to be much worse when you awaken in the middle of the night. When this happens, just tell yourself it will not be as bad in the morning. Yes, it is natural to worry, but it is also one of the most unproductive and destructive habits a person can possess.

It seems we lie more to ourselves than anyone else. Most of the things we fear and worry about never happen. Instead of worrying, change the subject and lullaby yourself to sleep by counting all the things you are grateful for: health, family, friends, and a paycheck. Remind yourself of the things you are proud of like your reputation, courage, volunteerism, optimism, and personal victories. You can pick it all up again in the morning, when things will look much better.

"Today is the tomorrow we worried about yesterday."
- Unknown

## Perseverance and Purpose

One of the most consistent characteristics of someone who is successful in the construction industry is perseverance. How many times do we have to pick ourselves up by our bootstraps and rise again after the defeats of not getting the next project, cost overruns and payment issues, irresponsible employees and irate customers? I have done this hundreds of times in my other career, and you will too if you want to succeed.

So go forward and persevere without fear. Make mistakes, pick yourself up, and then do it again and again. Don't agonize over the past: that is holding onto what you can't afford to keep. Learn from mistakes so you don't repeat them, knowing you will have opportunity to make new mistakes when you stop dwelling on the old ones.

Don't worry too much about what you cannot control in the future. Live in your positive imaginary future and not your negative past memory. Remember that behavior is a function of your decisions, not of your condition. Decisions come from values, but conditions come from feelings. If you choose to behave according to your feelings rather than your values, you will be reactive. Reactive people have less self-control and therefore empower the weakness in other people to control them.

Fulfill your dreams and remember your right to pursue happiness. Happiness is not the accumulation of material things but rather the measure of the value you bring to others and the value you create in the world. Many people who have accumulated a large amount of monetary wealth are also successful. Likewise, there are many wealthy people who are defeated.

Money, therefore, plays a minor role in the equation for success, because success is not the accumulation of things but instead to be the master of your values and principles. I believe that "personal values" are what you reflect on in determining what you believe to be right or wrong and also about how things should be.

Our personal values dictate why and how we behave or don't behave and the priority we give it. They are our perceived rules and ambition for what we believe is worthy, kind, important and wanted. Successful people value trustworthiness, dependability, loyalty and sincerity.

Your principles are your predetermined characteristic behaviors regarding your personal conduct and approach to taking action based on your values. They are a basic tenet about what you are willing to stand for and stand on.

I have not met anyone who is willing to die to protect their accumulations, but I do know people who have been willing to die to defend and protect their values and principles. Those are the people who place great value on protecting their families from harm and their country from its enemies. They do this on their own terms and within their hearts because they embrace family and freedom as their highest values and uphold their principles to do it.

It's about the willingness to stand on your own two feet under your high ethics and morals to respect someone as much as you respect yourself. You witnessed it on September 11, 2001, when firefighters and other rescuers ran into the burning World Trade Center Towers when others were running out. In witnessing the actions of the first responders, we all saw heroism on a level that the evil, inhuman attackers would be unable to conceive. The ethereal facial expressions displayed by the first responders trumped any personal trepidation of the impeding peril. I believe they entered knowing angels were by their side, and knowing for certain about their very near tragic future.

## Do Good

With life being always busy and time being always more compressed, why would you take your time and energy to do something for others?

You would do it because everyone has an obligation to help where you can or must. Sir Winston Churchill said: "We make a living by what we get, we make a life by what we give." Doing good for others is about unselfish reciprocity in giving what you have to those who do not have. It's not just about money but also about somehow lightening someone's load and doing something to make a positive difference in someone's life or in the world around you.

A couple of years ago, I had a conversation with two construction workers, Bill and Jim, who were working on the Interstate 35W in Minneapolis when it collapsed and fell into the Mississippi River on August 1, 2007. Thirteen people died and 145 were injured in that bridge failure.

I asked them what it was like and what they did. A little embarrassed, Bill explained, "Jim and I were standing behind a truck smoking a cigarette, when all of a sudden the bridge went down. After it crashed into the water it sprang back up a bit, and then dropped again. That spring effect threw Jim into the upstream water. He started to float back to me, screaming, 'Help! I'm going under the bridge!' I grabbed some rebar steel and hung it out over the water. He grabbed it and I pulled him up onto the crushed steel."

"Wow," I said. "What happened next? Did you run for your lives and get off the bridge and onto shore?"

They both said no. They proceeded to tell me that they stayed on the bridge, rescuing people who were stranded in their cars, people who were buried under structural steel and concrete, and people who were floating in the river.

"Weren't you afraid for your lives?" I asked.

Jim replied, "We were too busy to think about that."

You may not have the extreme opportunity to do for others what Bill and Jim did that day on the bridge. Nevertheless, keep in mind that doing good for others is what gives your life meaning. Giving is more about the support and benefit you are sending than about the pay you are receiving.

Unconditional giving in the construction industry is not as common as in nonprofit and volunteer organizations. Perhaps it's because we are more dependent on for-pay services and the practices of "I'll do a favor for you if you return one for me" and "If you want me to do this or that, then show me the money." However, unconditional giving to your fellow employees and to your customers is a character trait that is tied to empathy and is the key to the start and continuation of successful relationships.

> "Life's most persistent and urgent question is, 'What are you doing for others?'"
> - Reverend Martin Luther King, Jr.

## Share Your Gifts With People

I think it is fitting to conclude this book where it began. I dedicated this book to my younger brother Jim, for his courage and perseverance. Jim died at forty-nine, while I was writing this book. His death marked the end of a four-year battle with two forms of cancer. It also marked the beginning of a timeless memory of his heroic character and great bravery and perseverance. While he was in hospice I wrote and read the following letter to him. Hopefully this letter will provide the opportunity for you to realize the gifts we have and our responsibility to share them.

Jim:
There are many good people, some are great, and very few are considered best. You, Jim, are the best son, best brother, best husband, best uncle, best father and best friend. As you know, Mom calls you a saint and, although you are not formally canonized by the church, you do meet the official criteria of saintliness which includes being an exemplary model, morally admirable, devout and an extraordinary teacher of strength and perseverance.

Meeting those criteria is a result of your heroic character which is not something you can dream yourself into, but rather is a result of hammering and forging throughout your life . . . every day. You give people comfort by simply being there while you amaze them by going the extra mile even when no clear path is ahead of you. Stevie Wonder performed a song called "There's a Place in the Sun" and the words include, "Like an old dusty road/I get weary from the load . . . and before my life is done/I got to find me a place in the sun."

Jim, you found that place in the sun when you realized you didn't have the ability to control your health but did have the ability to script your life, all the while in the frustrating realization that the meaning of life is not an unquestionable answer but an unanswerable question. You did not ask for a lighter burden but rather for broader shoulders, while keeping your fears to yourself as you shared your courage with others. Your many gifts to us are forever valuable and include:

**Hope**: It's the walking dream of your faith, holding out your hand even while you are in the dark. Your gift of hope will sustain us that possibilities exist.

**Courage**: You did what you may have been afraid to do and it got you from one moment to the next. That gift is the ladder on which all other virtues mount.

**Persistence**: It was your quiet inner voice at the end of the day that said, "I will try this again tomorrow." That gift is knowing that one of the greatest glories is not in never falling, but in getting up every time we do.

**Humor**: The closest distance between two people, and a sure sign that you have a good grasp on life. Even when you were in treatment, humor was your instinct for taking pain playfully. You brought people together, including family, friends, and hospital staff for the simple purpose of laughter. Perhaps it was a part of your survival kit where you refused to be a tragic person even though in such an event. It's an affirmation of your dignity and your gift of knowing that humor allows our problems to slip away and be replaced with sunny spirits.

**Love**: For many people, love is just another word until someone like you comes around and gives it meaning. Your gift is to understand that to love and be loved is to feel the sun from both sides.

Jim, you have tremendous intrinsic worth which is an enormous source of inspiration and a treasured special gift to others. Nothing will have a greater lasting impression upon me than the awareness that you have transcended so much while holding and expressing those valued gifts that will always inspire others.

*-Joe*

If this book were a map, I believe the words would be easy to read and the directions would be simple to understand, but the actual route would not be simple. It would illustrate many challenging situations in an industry that requires the navigation of many ups, downs, roadblocks and blind spots as well as access to great opportunities and enduring relationships.

Successful travelers have the street smarts to know that both troublesome peril and fortunate prospect may be waiting around the bend. The itinerary for you, the navigator, is in the answer to the question about what route to select. Will you ascend to success or descend to failure? That ascent is more about the person than the environment, and going in either direction starts with the first step, so watch your steps.

Why? Because your employees and customers are watching too.

By now you understand that there is no magic wand. There is no big single secret to success. Instead, success is about doing many hundreds of things right and successfully managing the hundreds of things that go wrong. I hope this book helps you build or add to your success with the courage to seek it and the perseverance to recover from your failures. Remember that most worthwhile efforts contain risk. Risks can lead to failure, but going through failure brings success. Fix your mind not just on surviving in the industry but rather on attaining great success. And finally, remember that the road to success is always under construction.

Joe Egan

# About the Author

J oe Egan retired in 2005 after thirty-five years with the Egan Companies, one of the largest contractors in the nation. He spent his career in business development, customer relations, contract negotiations and conflict resolution on many large projects including power plants, hospitals, manufacturing facilities and office buildings.

Joe now works as sole proprietor of his consulting and seminar company, Egan Connection, LLC. and for his publishing company, Bridge Publications, LLC. He sat on the boards of the Egan Companies, St. Paul Builders Exchange, Minneapolis Builders Exchange, and Associated General Contractors of Minnesota. He currently sits on the advisory board for the Minnesota State University School of Construction Management.

He served as a supervisory training instructor and remains the annual convention chairman for Associated General Contractors of Minnesota. He was a Minnesota Health Care Hero nominee in 2010 and involved with the North Memorial Healthcare Foundation. He is the education coordinator at Twin Cities Healthcare Engineers Association and received their 2011 achievement award.

He has been with his wife for thirty-seven years, volunteers for Santa Claus visits to military families during the holidays, and is an assistant captain in the Minnesota Patriot Guard.

This is his first book.

MAR 16 2015

CPSIA information can be obtained at www.ICGtesting.com
Printed in the USA
LVOW13s0907150814

399255LV00018B/288/P